The Political
and
Moral Vision of Islam

S.H.M. JAFRI

Cover Photo:
Courtesy of Spaceimages.com
STS41-B McCandless MMU Distant Photo

Tahrike Tarsile Quran Inc.
Publishers & Distributors of the Holy Qur'an
80-08 51st Avenue
Elmhurst, New York 11373-4141

For legal and Copyright matters

In the name of God,
Most Gracious, Most Merciful

Published by

Tahrike Tarsile Qur'an, Inc.

Publishers and Distributors of the Holy Qur'an
80-08 51st Avenue
Elmhurst, New York 11373
www.koranusa.org
E-Mail: orders@koranusa.org

First U.S. Edition 2009

ISBN: 978-1-879402-25-6 Casebound
978-1-879402-26-3 Paperbound

Library of Congress Catalog Number: 2007926237

British Library Cataloguing in Publication Data

Printed in Canada

To
the Memory
of my Father

CONTENTS

FOREWARD

by Mahmoud M. Ayoub

The book *Nahj al-Balaghah* is one of the great spiritual and literary gems of Islam and the Arabic language. It consists of sayings, orations and letters of the Imam 'Ali Ibn Abi Talib, cousin and son-in-law of the Prophet Muhammad, in whose house he grew up in Islam, never having bowed his face to an idol. Thus, whenever 'Ali is mentioned, Muslims say, "May God magnify his face." The materials of this great book were collected and arranged by al-Sharif al-Radi [d. 405 A.H./1014 A.D.], himself a great poet, littérateur and religious scholar. Dr. S. H. M. Jafri presents in sophisticated, accurate and literary English three major texts from *Nahj al-Balaghah*: two letters from the Imam to two of his governors and his testimony (*wasiyyah*) to his son, the Imam al-Hasan. Dr. Jafri admirably represents the Imam's intention by presenting his words and profound thoughts to all Muslim readers, regardless of their *madhhab*, or legal school affiliation. May God reward Sayyid Jafri well for his noble effort; "*for God would not let the reward of those who do good be lost.*"

vi

PREFACE

The understanding of Islam in the West has a long and checkered history of more than a thousand years. It varies from a hostile attitude and a distorted perception to one of tolerance and rapprochement. In recent times however, there has been a renewed interest in Islam due to the changing geopolitical circumstances in general and certain economic, political and ideological factors related in Middle East specifically. After the tragic events of September 11, 2001 a sort of Islamophobia gripped the western world. Books, magazines, newspaper columns, editorials and most importantly, the powerful electronic media were employed to propagate a negative and distorted image of Islam. In most cases, Islam has been denied its Divine origin and spiritual character and has been described as a militant, violent, reactionary, fundamentalist, extremist and even a terrorist religion. This is contrary to all of the reconciliatory and sympathetic efforts made through inter-faith and inter-cultural dialogues, conferences, seminars and symposia in the 20th century held and hosted by a number of Western theological, ecumenical, social and cultural organizations. These positive efforts were further strengthened by the indepth and unbiased studies of some of the most renowned Western scholars of Islam including H.A.R. Gibb, A.J. Arberry, Louis Massignon and Annemarie Schimmel. Through their purely academic and objective approach they acknowledged and endorsed the Divine origin of Islam and its spiritual and ethical values. This should have enhanced the bond of mutual respect and recognition between the Islamic world and the West. Unfortunately, in spite of these efforts, divisive and negative forces prevailed and Islam has been looked upon with even greater suspicion than before, particularly in the past few decades.

Muslims, on the other hand have always recognized the Divine origin and spiritual character of Judaism and Christianity, never blaming these faiths for the misdeeds and heinous crimes committed by some of their followers, such as the immense sufferings of the Palestinians at the hands of the Zionists or the barbaric and inhuman act of bombing Hiroshima or Nagasaki by some Christians in which nearly 200,000 innocent men, women and children were killed. No religion can be blamed for the wrongs committed by some of its misled followers. Islam does not differentiate between any of the faiths, as is expressed very clearly in the Qur'an:

> *"Say (O Muslims), We believe in Allah and that which is revealed unto us and that which was revealed unto Abraham, and Ishmael, and Issac, and Jacob, and their tribes, and that which Moses and Jesus received, and that which Prophets received from their Lord. We make no distinction between any of them, and unto Him we have surrendered."* (The Qur'an, 2:130)

The most authentic and reliable way to know a religions tenets, fundamental beliefs and teachings is to carefully and objectively study its scripture, its history and what its proponents said and did. The fundamental source of Islam is the Qur'an, as exemplified in the sayings and teachings (*Sunna*) of the Prophet (Peace be upon him, pbuh). Much has been written in European languages including English on the Qur'an and the life and teachings of the Prophet (pbuh) of Islam, especially in modern times. There has, however not been enough material in these languages about the discourses and interpretations given by the closest disciples of the Prophet (pbuh). Interpretations and explanations of the early exponents of a religious tradition are very important in that they confirm, authenticate and validate the concepts, beliefs, teachings and practices of the religion for generations to follow.

This volume is a modest attempt to present three selections from the *Nahj al–Balagha* in English translation. A collection of sermons, sayings and documents of 'Ali bin Abi Talib, one of the closest disciples of the Prophet. Ali's place and position in early Islam and the importance and the authenticity of the *Nahj al–Balagha* have been discussed in detail in the second and the third chapters of this book., respectively. Two documents on "Conduct of Rule in Islam" provide the Islamic conception of justice and governance while the third, "Morality and Conduct of Life in Islam," gives an Islamic perspective on the importance of spiritual and ethical values in our materialistic world.

In the first chapter, 'Religion and State', I have tried to give a general outline of the relationship of religion and state and the major issues which comprise the core of all political philosophies throughout the ages. This will provide the reader with an opportunity to read Islam's political thoughts as explained by 'Ali bin Abi Talib, in comparison with different political philosophies before and after his time.

Now a word about the translation. I have tried to render the Arabic text into English as literally as possible, though often at the expense of flow and style. Wherever I found that strictly literal rendering does not fully convey the sense in English, I have added explanatory phrases in parentheses or explained such words in the footnotes.

For the Arabic text I have used mainly the edition of the *Nahj al-Balagha* extensively annotated by the great Egyptian scholar–reformer Shaykh Muhammad Abduh (d. 1905) and edited and published by Muhammad Ahmad Ashur and Ibrahim al-Banna. Although since then there have been many other editions of the *Nahj al-Balagha*, edited by distinguished scholars, I believe that for many reasons Shaykh Abduh's edition is still the best. He was a great lover and admirer of the *Nahj al-Balagha* and has paid his highest tributes to Ali in his preface to the book, for both the sublimity of his thoughts and the unparalleled beauty of his style and eloquence. As part of his campaign, Shaykh Abduh published the *Nahj al-Balagha* in about 1880, with his profound and scholarly comments and explanatory note for two reasons: firstly, to invite Muslims to ponder on Ali's thoughts on the fundamentals of Islam as well as on Islamic ideals and morality as explained by him; secondly, to remind the Arabs of their greatest literary heritage. To him, *Nahj al-Balagha* is one of the most beautiful models of Arabic literature and must be read with the highest esteem by the Arabs in memory of their glorious achievements in the past in the field of literature.

Before closing, it is my pleasant duty to thank Professor Mahmoud Ayoub of Temple University, U.S.A. for his valuable suggestions and for editing the manuscript: I also sincerely wish to thank Ms. Rukhsana Ali for her acceptance of the painstaking task of proofreading and for diligently preparing the manuscript for publication. Mr. Shakeeb Ahmed Khan typed the manuscript, I thank him too.

The Aga Khan University

S. H. M. Jafri
Karachi, Pakistan
27 September 2007

Section One

A Religio-Political Background

"And when you Judge between men,

Judge with Justice"

(The Quran, 4:58)

CHAPTER ONE

Religion and State in Islam

The political history of the Muslim Community can broadly be divided into four periods: (i) from the Hijra of the Prophet to Medina in 622 A.D., to the end of the Rashidun Caliphate in 661 A.D. (ii); from the establishment of the Umayyad dynasty in 661 A.D. to the ultimate collapse of the Muslim empires and states in the 18th–19th centuries; (iii) colonization and subjugation of Muslim states by Western imperial powers during the last two centuries and (iv) the reemergence of independent and sovereign Muslim states from the middle of the 20th century, which now number more than fifty. A thorough discussion of all these periods of the political history of the Muslim Community would require a separate volume. This introduction aims only to give an overview of the first Muslim state founded at Medina after the Prophet's migration to that city as well some passing reference to the subsequent periods. However, before discussing the first Muslim state in history, it may be helpful to note that there are two conflicting views on the function and nature of religion: one confines religion solely to the spiritual and ethical spheres, excluding the temporal and mundane aspects of life and society. The other claims for religion an all pervasive function which includes every aspect of human life, temporal as well as spiritual, worldly and other-worldly.

Indeed, no Prophet was sent to establish a state, an empire, a political authority or a governmental organization. The Qur'an speaks of only two Israelite prophets, David and Solomon, who also incidentally happened to be kings. But as is evident from the Qur'an itself, their kingship was due to certain historical circumstances and was not a part of their prophetic mission. David, a brave soldier, defeated the tyrant Goliath who had enslaved the Jews and in return the people, after the death of their king Saul, proclaimed him their king. Another Prophet-king, Solomon, as mentioned in the Qur'an simply inherited kingship from his father, David. But the Qur'anic emphasis on both of them is on their wisdom, righteousness and moral and ethical virtues, not on their kingship.[1]

The Prophet of Islam; the last of the Prophets, was called to prophethood in 610 A.D. at the age of forty to remind the people of their only 'Creator, Cherisher and the Most Bountiful' (whom man had forgotten). In fact, the first revelation contained in the first five verses of the *Sura al-Alaq* (96:1-5), calling the Prophet to his mission, epitomizes his *primary and fundamental* task of re-establishing man's relationship to his Creator, the ultimate source of all eternal values. Similarly, as the mission proceeded the Qur'an repeatedly kept reminding him of his *primary and fundamental duties*; that is, a) to pronounce the signs of God; b) to purify (the souls of men); c) to teach the Book and Wisdom; and d) to teach them what they do not know.[2] On the other hand, there is not the slightest indication in the Qur'an that it is also his duty to establish a state or a political authority as part of his prophetic mission.

Similarly, no religion comes to establish empires, states or political authorities. Prophets and religions are primarily intended to create a healthy society comprised of good, conscientious, virtuous, God-fearing and humane individuals. This is often described by the Qur'an as "*those who have faith and act virtuously*"[3] (*amanu wa 'amilu'l-salihat*). The society thus created, in turn creates its own institutions including the State, which reflect those positive qualities which the religion has inspired in it.

However, while the Qur'an defines the functions of the Prophets and religions as mentioned above, we must not ignore the fact that there is nothing in the Qur'an which prevents a Prophet from taking an active part in the temporal matters of the society in which he lives and carries out his mission. As a member of society, there are circumstances in which he cannot remain indifferent to the sociopolitical and economic problems of his people. As William Montgomery Watt points out: "the recent occidental conception of 'a purely spiritual movement' is exceptional. Throughout most of human history religion has been intimately involved in the whole life of man in society, and not least in his politics. Even the purely religious teaching of Jesus—as it is commonly regarded–is not without political relevance."[4] The most renowned French sociologist of religion, Emile Durkheim, emphatically declares: "the real function of religion... is to make us act, to aid us to live and that worship in its external form is a collection of the means by which this (the faith) is created and recreated periodically."[5] Durkheim even goes so far as to say that "religious ideas are collective ideas which represent collective realities."[6]

There is no doubt that as soon as we talk about ethical and moral values taught by a religion, it involves the entire life of man, spiritual as well as temporal. Moral and ethical values naturally manifest themselves not only in man's relationship to himself but also to his fellow human beings and to the society in which he lives. It was because of this relationship between religion and society that most Muslim scholars emphasize the unity of spiritual and temporal aspects in Islam. Thus Seyyed Hossein Nasr says: "Islam is the religion of unity, *tawhid* and all its functions, whether social or spiritual, are aimed towards the realization of this unity. Being the last of God's revelations, it symbolically reinstates man in his primordial state of *wholeness* in which the temporal and spiritual authorities were united within one body."[7] Fazlur Rahman, another most erudite Muslim scholar of modern times goes even further and describes Islam as a "faith-in-action." Comparing Islam with other monotheistic religions, he asserts: "For Muhammad's monotheism was, from the very beginning, linked up with a humanism and a sense of social and economic justice whose intensity is no less than the intensity of the monotheistic idea, so that whoever carefully reads the early revelations of the Prophet cannot escape the conclusion that the two must be regarded as expressions of the same experience."[8]

We do not contest these statements; however, what we wish to point out is that there is still some distinction between a Prophet's primary and fundamental mission as a teacher of spiritual and eternal values which never change and his participation in, or contribution to, temporal matters which are always subject to change. The former is eternal, primary and immutable and the latter is a part of history which always changes according to changing circumstances and man's experience in history.

It is with this distinction between the eternal and historical aspects of the teachings and actions of the Prophets that we may consider the first Muslim state, established at Medina under the direct supervision and guidance of the Prophet of Islam. However, it is not possible in these pages, nor it is desirable to go into any detail of the sociopolitical set up of North and Central Arabia including its two largest cities Mecca and Medina, the birth place and abode of Islam respectively. Suffice it to point out that it was deeply tribal in its sociopolitical structure and character and had no experience of a state or of governmental organization. Indeed Mecca at the time of the Prophet's birth was a strong commercial centre with a sort of commercial constitution and a council of elders, called *Mala'*, to settle disputes and to supervise and protect the commercial interests of the tribe. The city enjoyed peace because it was inhabited and controlled by only one powerful tribe, the Quraysh and also had a strong position because it housed the most prestigious sanctuary of the entire peninsula, the *Ka'ba*; of which they were the sole custodians. Yet, the city had no state authority or coercive powers to implement its decisions.

The situation of Medina, called Yathrib before Islam, was absolutely different from that of Mecca. It was inhabited by five warring tribes, three of them Jewish tribes: Banu Nadir, Banu Qaynuqa and Banu Qurayza and two Arab tribes of South Arabian origin, the Aws and the Khazraj. The Jews owned large estates of date-palms and were also engaged in handicrafts, while the Arab tribes mainly depended on their agricultural land. The Aws and Khazraj fought each other for a long time and the Jews, also divided among themselves, were supporting as allies one or the other feuding Arab tribes. It was thus the most unstable and unsafe city in the region. Unlike Mecca, it had no *Mala'* or council of elders to arbitrate inter-tribal wars or clan feuds. Thus the people of Medina were looking for some one who could impartially prevail upon the warring tribes and establish peace and tranquility in the city and save the people from continuous bloodshed.

It was this sociopolitical situation that attracted the people of Medina to the teachings of Islam and to the Prophet in whom they saw an impartial arbiter, a neutral judge as well as a Prophet possessing extraordinary wisdom to settle their disputes. It was therefore after two years of long and careful negotiations and the conversion of most, if not all of the two Arab tribes to Islam that the Prophet accepted their invitation to migrate to their city. They had to protect him from his enemies, the Quraysh and he had to give them peace and unity through spiritual fraternity.

Soon after the first pledge at al-Aqaba in 620 A.D., the Prophet started sending his Meccan followers to Medina and before he himself migrated in 622 A.D., he made it known that all the Meccan Muslims must migrate and settle down there. It was a carefully thought out strategy. He did not want to reach Medina as a fugitive, but as a chief of his own devoted followers from among the Quraysh, who numbered more than two hundred. Therefore, when he arrived at Medina he was enthusiastically received not only by his Medinan hosts; henceforth called the *Ansar* or helpers, but also by his own devoted Meccan followers, thereafter known as the *Muhajirs* or migrants.

After thirteen years of ceaseless effort, the Prophet at last succeeded in creating a full-fledged Muslim society which now could freely and openly practice its religion. In Mecca the Muslims were an outlawed minority, converted to a new religion and were socially, politically and economically under the domination of the non-Muslim majority of the Quraysh. In Medina, on the contrary they constituted a 'community' of their own in the true sense of the word. Once a community is established, it needs its own institutions including governmental organizations. Ibn Khaldun relates the rise of the state to that of society saying "the human need for society is not only natural but also necessary. Once society is formed there arises the need to maintain order and organizing social life. The state is therefore to society as form is to matter, for the form by its nature preserves the matter and... the two are inseparable."[9] Thus the newly formed Muslim Community composed of three different tribes from Medina and Mecca, divided into many clans had to evolve and adopt certain forms of political and governmental organization within which the constituent groups could live harmoniously. There were also three Jewish tribes living in Medina who constituted an important part of civil life of the city and must be duly accommodated along with the Muslims. In fact, the city of Medina was now inhabited by two equally important religious communities, Muslims and Jews. A third group, pagans who were allies of the aforementioned two communities may also be added here.

The Prophet therefore promulgated a treaty (*Mithaq*) commonly known as the constitution of Medina, binding all the three Muslim tribes and their clans for the closest possible cooperation with one another and with the Jews. The treaty consists of 52 clauses in which clause two is repeated 20 times either in full or in a shorter form with the name of the group which entered into the agreement at different dates being changed.[10] It should be noted that the treaty was signed independently by various clans and not by the tribes as a whole. However, the remaining 32 clauses can be divided in two parts; one dealing with the affairs of the Muslims alone and the other detailoing the joint responsibilities of Muslims and Jews as equal citizens of the state. The treaty also includes the pagans living in or around Medina who had been in alliance with any of the Muslim or Jewish clans. It is not essential to give full the text of the document here, so only those points which deal jointly with both the Muslims and the non-Muslims will be mentioned. Ibn Ishaq introduces the document in the following words:

> "The Messenger of God (God bless and preserve him) wrote a document (*Kitab*) between the migrants and the Helpers (*Ansar*) in which he made a treaty and covenant with the Jews, confirmed them in their religion and properties, some conditions were laid down on them and they were bound by some conditions."[11]

After Ibn Ishaq's introduction, the document commences with the following preamble:

> "In the name of God, the Merciful, the Compassionate! This is a document from Muhammad the Prophet [governing the

relations] between the believers and Muslims of Quraysh and Yathrib and those who followed them and are attached to them and who strive along with them (i.e. the Jews and their allies)."[12]

What follows are the main points concerning the relationship between the two communities and their rights and duties as indicated in the preamble:

1. Muslims and Jews should live as one people. They are a single community (*Ummatun Wahida*), to the exclusion of all other peoples.

2. The migrants of Quraysh shall pay the blood-money jointly between them according to their former customs; and they shall ransom their captives with uprightness and justice between the believers (they shall decide their disputes according to their tribal customs). This clause is repeated twenty times either in the same words or in a shorter form, with only the name of the signatory being changed.[13]

3. Each party practice its own faith and neither should interfere with that of the other.

4. In the event of war with a third party, each should come to the assistance of the other, provided the latter were the party aggrieved and not the aggressor.

5. In the event of an attack on Medina, both should participate in its defense.

6. Peace should be made only after consultation with each other.

7. Medina should be regarded as sacred by both the parties, and all bloodshed forbidden therein.

8. No pagan is to give protection to any person of the Quraysh— neither to his goods or his person, or take side part in hostilities against any believer (in this way even pagans are clearly included in the treaty).

9.   The Prophet would be the final court of appeal to settle disputes (if the parties concerned are unable to solve the problem).

The other 23 clauses deal exclusively with the various obligations and responsibilities of the Muslim tribes and clans as members of a single community of believers.[14]

The constitutions of states are inextricably linked to the geographical, social, cultural and economic realities of the land and the people. A state, as we have seen earlier, is a moderating factor in a society torn by conflicting interests and its constitution responds to the demands made by the nature of the conflicts and their intensities. The form and the nature of a constitution are also determined by the relationships between different sections and classes of people. The constitution of the first Muslim state of Medina was not exception and was a natural corollary to the realities and traditions of its times and its society. Yet the Prophet succeeded in introducing a revolutionary change in the Arab's concept of civil life. So far the whole concept of tribal life was based on the bond of blood, now the emphasis had been shifted to a community constituted through a freely accepted pact which became more binding than tribal ties. Nicholson admiringly comments on the constitution, saying:

> "No one can study it (constitution) without being impressed by the political genius of its author. Muhammad does not strike, openly at the independence of the tribes, but he destroyed it, in effect, by shifting the centre of power from the tribe to the community; and although the community included Jews and pagans as well as Muslims, he fully recognized, what his Opponents fail to foresee, that the Muslims were the active, and must soon be the predominant, partners in the newly founded state."[15]

The word 'destroy' used by Nicholson seems to be rather too strong. The Prophet did not and in fact could not destroy the independence of the tribes, but he brought it under the supreme interest of the community which now stood over and above every other interest. In the final analysis however, the following points of the constitution are the most prominent: (1) the emergence of a political, pluralistic nation irrespective of religious, ethnic or tribal affiliations; (2) it guarantees complete religious freedom; therefore, it is liberal in its function; (3) it gives complete internal freedom to all of its constituent clans and tribes and thus it is federal in its character; and finally, (4) allegiance and loyalty to the community supersedes any other loyalty.

With these characteristics of its foundational constitution the first Muslim state came into being in 622 A.D., the year of the Hijra and also that of the beginning of the Muslim calendar. The Prophet was certainly the undisputed head of state; and equally undisputedly, he was the head of the state because he was the Prophet. Otherwise, he would have been only the chief of his emigrant Qurayshite followers, like the other chiefs of the respective clans and tribes of Medina. However, it is exactly this point which has created serious confusion of far-reaching consequences for the Muslim Community. The question of whether he was head of the state as a part of his prophetic mission or because as the recipient of revelation he was the wisest, the most competent and the most trusted man on earth at the time and therefore, in the presence of such a person, who else would be better suited to be head of state, was not objectively analyzed. Two obvious facts in connection to this question may lead to a better understanding of the Prophet's position as the head of the Medinan state. One, the constitution of Medina as referred to above clearly represents the particular socio-cultural and geo-economic conditions of a tribal society at a particular time in history. Thus the state and the constitution promulgated by the Prophet belonged to a particular milieu and not to what we would call the eternal and immutable teachings of Islam. Two, according to the Sunni theory of caliphate, the Prophet did not clearly nominate his successor, instead leaving it to the community to select its chief. It meant that he did not interfere in the deep-rooted North and Central Arabian custom of selecting a new chief at the death of the previous one. This again shows that the newly founded state of Medina belonged to the community and its sociopolitical requirements, not to the religion as such. This is further evinced by 1) the way the first four caliphs, known as the Rashidun, were chosen; and 2) the laws and administrative code they adopted in governing the state and affairs of the people.

The first caliph, Abu Bakr was selected even before the burial of the Prophet, in the public hall of Medina, Saqifa Banu Sa'ida, after heated debates and altercations between the leaders of the *Ansars* and the *Muhajirun*. Detailed accounts of the arguments and counterarguments put forward by the two contesting groups for leadership of the community are preserved by numerous early sources. None of them reports that a single verse of the Quran or any religious argument was advanced by either party in support of their claims. The entire debate concentrated on the sociopolitical requirements of the community.[16] The only tradition of the Prophet quoted at the occasion says that "the leaders are from the Quraysh" (*al-aimmat-u min al-Quraysh*). This tradition, if so accepted signifies only socio-political constraints and realities rather than any religious requirements or implications. Thus the selection of the first caliph was made according to the traditions of North and Central Arabia. This somehow satisfied the challenges confronting the nascent state at the sudden demise of the Prophet.

The first caliph, after a short rule of about two years, nominated 'Umar b. al-Khattab as his successor while on his deathbed.[17] This was apparently a deviation from both the old traditions and also from the precedent set by the Prophet, who did not nominate his successor. The first caliph, in his political insight of the given situation thought it expedient not to leave the choice so wide open as did the Prophet at his time and decided to make arrangements for his succession. This proves how drastically the requirements of the fledgling state changed in just two years time; otherwise Abu Bakr would not have deviated from tradition. However the second caliph, after ten years of rule, found it in the best interests of the state to deviate from the precedents set by the Prophet and by his predecessor, appointing a committee consisting of six companions of the Prophet to select one from among themselves as the new caliph,[18] introducing yet another method of selection. As a result, 'Uthman b. al-'Affan, one of the members of the committee, was selected as the third caliph. After twelve years of rule, he met with a tragic, violent death at the hands of rebels from Egypt, Kufa and Basra[19] and thus had no opportunity to make any arrangements for his succession. 'Ali b. Abi Talib was therefore compelled by the companions and multitudes of the people assembled in Medina to become the fourth caliph.[20] Ali's caliphate lasted barely five years; he too was assassinated in 661 A.D. This was the end of the Rashidun caliphate, the state of Medina and the beginning of a long period of dynastic, monarchic, imperial and often despotic, oppressive and dictatorial rule to last until the colonization of the Muslim states in the 18th–19th centuries.

On what theoretical principles the first four 'pious' caliphs were selected was not defined at the time of their selection. Apparently, all of these different methods were dictated by the exigencies of time and the circumstances of their historical context. It was long after their selection that Muslim political theorists like al-Mawardi (d. 1058) termed to these various methods as 1) *ijma* (consensus), 2) *nass* (nomination), 3) *shura* (consultation), and again 4) *ijma*, respectively.[21] Which of these three methods adopted by the 'rightly guided' caliphs in their political or pragmatic wisdom is to be taken as specifically Islamic? The simple answer is that no religion, including Islam has ever given a fixed system, form or structure for government, as it is a matter for human experience and circumstances. However, religion in general and Islam in particular, is indeed interested in the substance and conduct of rule; but that as an element of its moral and ethical teaching in general and not as a blueprint for state policy, as we shall see presently.

Let us now make a brief reference to the laws and administrative code the Rashidun caliphs adopted for running the state bequeathed to them by the Prophet. Indeed, their first and foremost source of law had been the Qur'an and the *Sunna* of the Prophet. However, the rapid expansion of Muslim rule into vast areas of the Byzantine and Persian empires with their peoples of different social, cultural, ethnic, economic, religious and philosophical backgrounds, created many new and unprecedented problems for the caliphs to deal with. For most of these new problems, there was nothing either in the Qur'an or in the *Sunna* and the caliphs had to resort to their own judgment, called *ijtihad*. In their pragmatic wisdom and sagacity, they freely, unhesitantly and liberally adopted from what ever source they could find any thing suitable in a given situation. Thus much of the laws and administrative systems of the Byzantine and Persian provinces were incorporated into the caliphal administration, provided they were not in conflict with the socio-economic justice and fundamental principles of Islam. These laws, taken from many divergent sources, in the course of time became part of the *Shari'a* but also sources of *Shari'a* law.[22]

Keeping in mind the i) nature and character of the constitution of Medina; ii) pragmatism rather than fixed principles in selection of the first four caliphs; and iii) liberal adaptation of laws and systems from so many alien sources–the question that arises is, by what theoretical or ideological name should refer to the first Muslim State of Medina founded by the Prophet? Should we call it theocratic or secular, democratic or socialist, liberal or totalitarian? The most important fact which must be kept in mind in this regard is that all of these ideological terms with their underlying political and economic implications are western and also modern, dating mainly from the 17th century onward. Equally important is the fact that there is no equivalent for any of these terms in pre-Islamic, Qur'anic, Prophetic, classical or medieval Arabic language. Even now, these terms in Arabic or Persian are adopted from other languages. However, let us examine two of these terms in connection with the first Muslim State of Medina.

The most important of these terms in relation to Islam is theocracy. The word was coined in the Greek language (*Theokratia*) by the Jewish historian Josephus Flavius around 100 AD. Josephus noted that while the nations of the world were governed by monarchies, oligarchies or democracies, the polity of the Jews was a theocracy. This, he thought, went back to Moses, who was not attracted to these other models and therefore "designated his government a theocracy as someone might say, forcing an expression - thus attributing the rule and dominion of God" (Against Apion 2.165). However, since Josephus's coinage the term theocracy found its expression in various forms and meanings: a) hierocracy, or rule of religious functionaries; b) royal theocracy or rule by a sacred king; c) general theocracy, or rule in a more general sense by divine will or law; and d) eschatological theocracy, or future rule by a divine.[23] In 1622, the term was used by the poet John Donne stating that Jews had been under a theocracy. The *Shorter Oxford Dictionary* explains the term as "a form of Government in which God (or a deity) is recognized as the king or immediate ruler, and his laws are taken as the statute-book of the kingdom; these laws are being usually administered by a priestly order as his ministers and agents; hence (loosely) a system of government by a sacerdotal order, claiming a divine commission." In 1825, it was further defined as "a priestly order or religious body exercising political or civil power."[24] It was precisely in this sense of priestly rule that theocracy appeared in the Papal States of medieval Europe and lasted for over a millennium from 756 to 1870. European states were thus controlled by the church; priests were the functionaries of the state, the Pope in Rome being the central authority.[25]

Islam has never been a theocracy in any of the four forms mentioned above, even during the life time of the Prophet or his immediate successors. Before we comment further on this, we would like to quote Taha Husain, an eminent Egyptian scholar, from Asghar Ali Engineer's book, *The Islamic State*, in connection with the Qur'anic verse *"And consult them (those around you) in affairs of [moments]"* (3:159). "Taha Husain .... quotes the above verse to show that the state founded by Muhammad (pbuh) was not a theocratic state. He maintains that nothing can be more misleading than the concept that the state founded by the Prophet of Islam was a theocratic state. Islam, after all is a religion which emphasizes the unity of God, the Prophethood (of Muhammad) and righteous living. It draws attention to this and to otherworldly life but it does not deprive human beings of their freedom and it (Islam) does not become an absolute master of man nor does it suspend his initiative to act. Islam instead makes him the master within certain limits. It showed what was desirable and what was repulsive and of course, it laid emphasis on reason and gave freedom (with the help of reason) to think what was good and in the interest of common people and to take part in the common good to the extent possible. God commanded the

Prophet to consult the faithfuls in (their) affairs. If everything is to be decided in the heavens, there is no need to consult anyone."[26]

Taha Husain's argument is both rational and theological and makes his point absolutely clear. We have presented historical evidence from the constitution of Medina promulgated by the Prophet himself which was liberal in every respect, giving every citizen freedom of religion as well as freedom of practicing their tribal laws and customs. We also referred to the pragmatic and practical methods with which the immediate successors of the Prophet were chosen without citing any religious injunction. We also explained that the caliphs liberally and unhesitantly adopted alien laws and codes to run the state. Not only this, the Pious caliphs sometimes even did not apply the clear injunctions of the Qur'an and the *Sunna* because in their religious and practical insight, the welfare of the people in a given situation demanded it.[27] With these historical facts and the theological and rational argument put forward by Taha Husain, it is rather difficult to assert that the Medinan state founded by the Prophet and run by the Rashidun caliphs for thirty years was a theocracy, notwithstanding that the Qur'an and the *Sunna* remained the supreme law.

In connection with the term theocracy, a word in passing regarding the concept of sovereignty of God and the viceregency of man is necessary. Some Muslim religio-political ideologies, especially in modern times try to interpret the sovereignty of God and viceregency of man in political terms. First of all, it must be remembered that the idea of the political sovereignty of God was first propounded by the Church in the historical context of medieval Europe. In Europe before 756 A.D., the legitimacy of rule was derived from kingship by birth, acquisition by force or by an Athenian or Roman style democracy. It was against this background that the Church propounded the theory of the Sovereignty of God in all human affairs including the state. In this way the Church legitimized its political authority and appropriated state control and political rule for itself for more than a millennium.

In the Qur'an, on the other hand all of those verses which refer to the Sovereignty of God mean that He is the Creator and Supreme ruler of the universe and that the entire cosmic order is governed and directed by His will and wisdom. This divine will is equivalent to the laws of nature, which are immutable.[28] It is in this sense that the Qur'an talks about the Sovereignty of God which is supreme in the earth and the heavens: "*to God belongs what is in the heavens and the earth*" (24:4). Thus to argue that the absolute and universal Sovereignty of God operates in the affairs of man in the same way as in the working of nature is extremely questionable. As far as the assertion that man is the vicegerent of God on earth and thus has been given the authority to rule as his representative is a rather far-fetched interpretation of these verses of the Qur'an.

The idea of the political authority of man is derived from the word *Khalifa* or its plural *Khulafa* or *Khalaif* which means the one who takes the place of some one before him. It is in this meaning that the word *Khalifa* occurs in many verses of the Qur'an. Two verses in particular are cited to prove the political viceregency of man on earth. One refers to David; we have disccussed this verse already. More commonly and emphatically cited is a verse relating the creation of Adam which reads:

> "*And when thy Lord said unto the angels, I am about to make a viceregent (*Khalifa*) in the earth, They said, 'Wilt Thou place therein one who will do evil therein and shed blood? Whereas we celebrate Thy praise and sanctify Thee.' Said He. I know what you know not. And He taught Adam all the names, then showed them to the angels saying: inform me of the names of these, if ye are truthful. They said: Be glorified: We have no knowledge except that which Thou hast taught us. Behold: Thou only art the knower, the wise. He said: 'O Adam: inform them of their names ...'*" (2:30-33).

These three verses are very clear about the position of man on earth and are self-explanatory. Firstly, it states that God wanted to inform the angels that He was going to create a new being, Adam and his progeny. This is evident from the text; for when the angels heard this announcement they asked God whether He would replace them with one (Adam) who was potentially an evil-doer, while they were innocent.

The verse therefore signifies only the advent of man on earth. Secondly, from the text it is also clear that the whole human is meant and not a particular individual. In the words of Allama Iqbal, "the word Adam is retained and used as a concept than as the name of a concrete human individual." Iqbal quotes another verse of the Qur'an to support his point saying: "The use of the word [Adam in the meaning of human race] is not without authority in the Qur'an itself. The following verse is clear on the point: *We created you, then fashioned you, then said We to the angels, 'Prostrate yourself unto Adam'*" (7:11).[29]

Thirdly, the last verse clearly shows Adam's (man's) superiority over the angels in acquisition of knowledge and as explained by Iqbal, "in remembering and reproducing the names of things. The purpose of these verses as I have shown before, is to bring out the conceptual character of human knowledge."[30] At another place Iqbal says: "It is the lot of man to share in the deeper aspirations of the universe around him and to shape his own destiny as well as that of the universe, now by adjusting himself to its forces, now by putting the whole of his energy to mould its forces to his own ends and purposes. And in this process of progressive change *God* becomes a *Co-worker with him*, provided man takes the initiative"[31] (emphasis is mine). Man is thus potentially higher than angels in knowledge and he is a synthesis from which no element, from the highest to the lowest, is excluded. He unites in himself the divine and the earthly and it is precisely in this sense that man can be defined as *Khalifat Allah fi'l-ard*, the viceregent of God on earth.

The word *Khalifa* is also used in the Qur'an in a number of other verses where it simply means that one people have succeeded another people and one generation another generation. We may now conclude that from the word *Khalifa* as used in the Qur'an, no political doctrine or theory of caliphate can be deduced. And in fact, the political theories drawn from the Qur'an have been dictated either by political exigencies, or later judicial and theological necessities, especially during the Abbasid dynasty who unlike the Umayyads, claimed for themselves religious leadership as well.

We have seen above that the Muslim state cannot be called a theocracy in the sense of the Papal states. Should we then call it secular? We will try not to give our views on this rather complex subject which has, unfortunately become quite sensitive in certain Muslim circles. The term as a particular political ideology initially came into being as a reaction to the temporal authority of the church. Its meaning as irreligiosity or *ladiniyat* is now almost a ghost of a meaning belonging to a particular historical background. This ghost meaning somehow continues among the Muslims in particular without the realization that the term itself has gone through many changes in its historical development. We will therefore restrain ourselves to quoting from some of the Christian authorities and then leave it to the reader to arrive at their own conclusions. In the *Encyclopedia Britannica* it is defined as follows:

> A movement in society directed away from other worldliness to this-worldliness. In the medieval period there was a strong tendency for religious persons to despise human affairs and to meditate on God and the afterlife. As a reaction to this medieval tendency, secularism exhibited itself in the development of humanism during the Renaissance, when man began to show more interest in human cultural achievements and the possibilities of his fulfillment in the world. The movement toward secularism has progressed ever since, often being viewed as anti-Christian and anti-religious in nature. In the latter half of the 20th century, a number of theologians began advocating secular Christianity. They suggested that *Christianity should be concerned not only with the sacred and the otherworldly, but rather that man should find in the secular world the opportunity to promote Christian values. These theologians maintain that the real meaning of the message of Jesus can be discovered and fulfilled in the every day affairs of secular urban living* (emphasis added).[32]

This explains that the term was first used as a reaction to certain religious tendencies in the medieval period and was not meant to denote an anti-religious outlook.

Barkes Niyazi explains it as, "the term Secularism signifies that which is not religious. It is rooted in the Latin world *Seculum*, which initially meant *"age"* or *"generation" in the sense of temporal time*. It later became associated with matters of this world, as distinct from those of the spirit directed toward attainment of Paradise"[33] (emphasis is mine).

Lastly, Charles D. Smith, in his article "Secularism" in the *Oxford Encyclopedia of Modern Islamic World*, quoting E.G.. Hobsbawm and Glasner says: "In the European historical experience, which itself varied widely, *the secularization process coexisted with an intensification of religiosity on the personal and popular level.* Some sociologists argue... *that aspects of secularism and religiosity always coexisted and still do. Secularization did not mean a necessary erosion of religious belief* either in the pre-industrial age or the industrial. *Religious belief and practice, as faith, intensified rather than declined during the secularization* of the State and later, following the French and Industrial Revolution, that of society" (Hobsbawm). It continues, "Religion today coexist with industrial, technically secular society and intensified its activities in the United States where in official circles it is considered an almost essential part of being American"[34] (Glasner). These are the most authentic and contemporary interpretations of secularism as it is understood and practiced in the West. The meaning of the word as *age* or *generation* is particularly important, indicating its relevance in a 'time-space' context.

A careful analysis of the modern Western concept of secularism as quoted above clearly shows that there is no antagonism between religious and secular, spiritual and temporal, sacred and profane. Indeed both spheres, though complimentary to each other are different and must be so by their very nature. Man is the Creation of God and therefore divine and primordial in his origin; as He says: "*and I breathed into him of my spirit*" (15:29), whereas the state is the creation of man and transient and must remain open to change as necessitated by history or geography.

The political history of the Muslims from the earliest times until now is full of instances where the Islamic State adopted foreign laws, administrative systems and customs. We have already quoted the constitution of Medina where the tribes were allowed to follow their pre-Islamic laws and customs to solve internal problems. The second caliph 'Umar bin al-Khattab, when asked by his officers appointed on the border of Persian and Byzantine empires how to charge custom duty from the traders coming to Muslim territory, the caliph replied: "charge them as they charge your traders." This is only one out of hundreds of such examples from the Rashidun caliphate. Many Byzantine and Persian laws and administrative procedures, as we have seen earlier, were assimilated into the legal and administrative system of the Muslim state. Later when North Africa, Spain, India and other foreign lands came under Islamic rule, the local laws and rules of these countries were incorporated into Islamic administration. This process continued throughout Islamic political history and introduced a great deal of heterogeneity into Islamic law and played no small role in the secularization of Islamic law as well as governmental organization and policy.

In short, secularism in political terms means that a government is not committed to any *particular sect or group*. In other words, secularism denotes only that the State does not and should not favor any particular community in matters of religion and that no particular religion should impose its ideology and its way of life on the followers of other religions. "In this sense it is in accordance with the Islamic tradition which gives religious freedom to every citizen. This is the meaning in which secularism is being practiced in secular countries, and the Muslims too should not see any conflict between their religion Islam, and secularism."[35] Secularism today for all practical purposes is not anti-religion, it is only anti-communalism.

We have discussed the concepts of religious polity (or theocracy) and secularism since the entire Muslim *Umma* is entangled in this controversy. In almost every Muslim state, one group insists on purely religious dispensation of the affairs of state while the other strongly advocates that the state, by necessity, must be secular. Except for the Muslims, all other nations have found a happy reconciliation between religion and secular administration though they may be divided by other conflicting political ideologies. There is capitalism, socialism, communism and

21

democracy of divergent interpretations, ranging from totalitarianism to that of unlimited liberalism, each claiming to be the sole custodian of human welfare and claiming that it alone can bring happiness and socio-economic justice to mankind.

The Muslim states, now free from the colonial yoke and once again the masters of their own affairs and destinies, are also in search of a political system with which they can re-establish their political identity. But unlike the Chinese or the Indians who derive their identity from their land, common history and ancient cultures and unlike the Western nations who derive their political ideals from Graeco-Roman tradition and thought, Muslims have emerged as a religio-political community which depends on the basic principles of their religion for their political identity.

Historically, the medieval political system with which the Muslims governed their states and empires has not only already collapsed but its weaknesses made them easy prey to the foreign powers. Since the establishment of the Umayyads rule in 661 A.D. (41 A.H.); just forty years after the death of the Prophet until today, the political history of the Muslims has been nothing but the history of despotic kings, monarchs, sultans, and military dictators. Thus disappointed with their own political past and equally unwilling to adopt any of the modern political ideologies, Muslims have found themselves in a vacuum and in a state of utter confusion. This has led them to turn to Islam for guidance and inspiration. However, the urge for the reassertion of an Islamic political identity has so far expressed itself only in empty slogans. Whereas all other contemporary ideologies or systems have been effectively implemented and have long been in actual practice with results good or bad, the Muslims have so far done hardly anything tangible in the modern world. In actual practice, as has been pointed out; after the initial phase of four decades in Medina, Muslims have never shown the world what the Islamic system of government really should have been, nor have they done any serious work during the long centuries of their history.

Islam did provide a model state in Medina, on which an elaborate system could have been developed, adapting from time to time to changing circumstances according to the demands of the times. The Muslims failed to do so at that time; but if the West after centuries of slumber and moral and political decadence could turn to its classical period for renewed inspiration in the Renaissance, the Enlightenment and the Reformation periods, why cannot Muslims in their own search for political identity or rejuvenation turn to the pristine source of Islam for inspiration with the genuine spirit of *ijtihad*? This should not, however, be confused with what today is called 'fundamentalism' in the reactionary sense. The term has many shades of meaning, depending on the historical context and the background against which it is used. If fundamentalism means literalism or rigid and strict adherence to the letter even in the mundane, social aspects of a religious tradition, as has been the case with a small group of followers in every religion, it would lead to confusion and incompatibility with the demands imposed by changing circumstances. If, on the other hand, it means to resort to the original and fundamental teachings of a religion and its basic and normative principles for guidance, then it cannot be called fundamentalism in the narrower sense as it is generally understood. If so, the movements of the Renaissance, the Reformation and the Enlightenment may also be called fundamentalism through which the West rid itself of the ills of the middle ages and derived inspiration and guidance from its classical heritage. Similarly the Muslims, caught between the ills of their own medieval political history and alien political ideologies, have now turned to Islam to rediscover those guiding and normative principles which can help them in their urge to reestablish and reassert their political identity. Originally, Islam was neither theocratic nor secular in the modern sense of these terms. To revive Muslim society and to establish its own distinctive character, there must be a revival of this original spirit of Islam and at the same time, an incorporation of the best that has been developed by others, as indeed it did in its early stage. By original spirit we mean *ijtihad* and a liberal approach and attitude with which the Muslims of earlier times absorbed whatever good they found in any culture. The basic principles of Islam which we have referred to are explained by Iqbal in the following words:

"The essence of Tauhid, as a working idea, is equality, solidarity, and freedom. The State, from Islamic standpoint, is an endeavour to transform these ideal principles into *Space-time forces*, an aspiration to realise them in a definite human organization."[36]

What Iqbal calls, "space-time forces," is almost the same as Barkes Niyazi's explanation of secularism as quoted above which initially meant "age" or "generation" in the temporal sense.

However, since our main purpose is to present Ali's thoughts on the function of the state, we have examined in some detail the first phase of the political history of Islam as a particular background. Still, there are some major issues of political philosophy which must be mentioned to in order to elucidate his ideas about the state and society in general. The nature and function of a state is determined by the social ideas and the political philosophy on which it is founded. These philosophies, from the times of Plato and Aristotle (the first systematic thinkers on politics) to our own time differ considerably from each other. But in all political theories three major elements constitute the basis of political thought. The nature and function of man; his relation to the rest of the universe which determines the meaning of life as a whole; and emerging from the relation of these two, the problem of the relation of man to his fellow men. The last is the main concern of political theory in the narrowest sense and articulates the nature, purpose and function of the state. These three factors, man, his ultimate goal and his social life and responsibilities, are in constant interaction with each other, being reflected in varying degrees in political thought, particularly the concept of the state.

The most difficult and indeed, the most complex question has been the nature of man himself, around which all other questions revolve; a question which has divided the thinkers of all ages. Some deem man sinful; others give him no moral freedom of choice and reduce him to an automaton. One group of thinkers will consider him a creature of irrational impulse and passion while the other will credit him with reason. As the nature of man is variously understood and interpreted over time, so is the shift in the understanding of the function of the state by political thinkers.

However, as soon as the function of the state is discussed, the authority which the state may claim to exercise over its members becomes an unavoidable question to be decided. No state can function without having authority and power vested in it. The nature of sovereignty, which may be said to reside in any state, determines the nature of political obligation. Why and how far should a man obey the dictates of the society and the state in which he lives? Is it a moral or societial duty to be obedient; if so, on what grounds? From what sources does the state derive its legitimacy to rule and impose its will?

Underlying political obligation is the subject of law. When a man questions his duty to obey, he is also criticizing the law he is called on to obey. He inquires into the nature of law; whether it is fundamental, infallible, immutable and unchangeable by any endeavor of man; or whether it has been established by man and as such is fallible and mutable. The nature of authority, the nature of political obligation and the nature of law are thus interdependent questions.

Arising from these there are three other problems which cannot be avoided while discussing the concept and function of a state; namely, justice, equality and liberty. From the classical period of the Greek thinkers down to our own times and in all political systems, these three questions have been the most pressing. Every state or form of government, past or present, ranging from totalitarian dictatorships to that of liberal democracies, have always claimed to be the best dispenser of these necessary virtues. These three aspects are, however, so interwoven with each other that it is impossible to deal with one in isolation from the others. However, as far as the question of justice is concerned, it must receive our particular attention for two reasons: firstly, it is one of the most important functional requirements of any polity and secondly, in Islam it has a central position not only in connection with the state but as a fundamental doctrinal principle. One of the fundamental attributes of God in Islam is the attribute of justice which must by necessity be reflected in every sphere of human life and every human institution, the state being the most important.

The concept of justice as it is generally interpreted by political thinkers is a relative term and is difficult to define in an absolute sense. We hear of retributive justice, distributive justice, social justice, legal justice and political justice, each with its own implications and requirements, but hardly of justice alone as an abstract virtue. According to the ancient definition which is still perhaps the nearest to a comprehensive conception of justice, a society or state is just if it renders to its various members what is due to them or what is their right.[37] This in turn raises the question of what it is that is their due. We may specify that their due is what is laid down by the laws of the state. The laws of the state, however, may themselves be unjust and if so, it follows that justice cannot consist wholly in their observance. Since justice includes moral as well as legal justice, one might say that a society is just if its laws and actions conform to its moral standards. But even the prevailing moral principles of a society may be unjust and oppressive as, for example, in the case of medieval Europe or pre-Islamic Arabia.

It may be said that a man's due or his right is that which is his by virtue not merely of the law or of the prevailing moral rules but of *valid* moral principles; a society is then just if it accords its members what it is required to accord them by *valid* moral principles. By this interpretation, justice consists of the most opportune balance of good and evil, reward and punishment, privileges and opportunities, all in accordance with moral principles which are valid. To this few if any would disagree. But what are those moral principles which are *valid* and by what criteria and on what authority? Are there some moral principles or criteria which can be universally applicable and acceptable? We will not try to answer these questions here, as the documents we will present deal with them adequately.

What has been said so far about the meaning and the concept of justice would in the final analysis mean that a society or a state must treat all of its members with equality; or in legal terms, every one should be equal before the law. This as it is makes justice and equality twin concepts. The inseparable relationship between justice and equality has always been manifested throughout human history. The great historic struggles for justice have always centered around demands for equal rights: the struggles against slavery, despotic rule, domination of one group over another, political absolutism, economic exploitation, the accumulation of wealth in a few hands, the disfranchisement of the poor and lower class, discrimination based on caste, creed and color, racial oppression and monopolies of all sorts. Aristotle unequivocally declared that "justice is equality."[38] The demand for equality is built into the very concept of justice—and justice cannot exist without taking the equal rights of the people into consideration. The just society or state must then consider and protect the 'good life' of each man equally, no matter how different these men may be and as such must allow them equal consideration, equal opportunity and equality before the law.

Finally, the third component of the triumvirate, the concept of liberty is perhaps more complex than either justice or equality, in both conceptual interpretation and in its practical aspect. It involves a thorough examination of the nature and character of an individual, his relation to the society in which he lives and acts and his relation to the state of which he is a citizen. Liberty stresses the exemption of the individual from governmental restraints, while collective or social life demands the formal framework of the rule of law and certain restrictions whereby men are entitled to equality before the law and to equal protection by the law. It is very well to say that individual freedom should be maximized but without certain restraints imposed by positive law and governmental control, human life becomes impossible.[39] But what is the just extent of such restraints? Is there any principle which determines the area within which men may be free to do as they wish without restraint from any external source? What is the source of legitimacy of the authority which can impose restraints on an individual? These questions have always been perplexing for political thinkers, resulting in different and often contradictory ideologies. However, the liberty man needs is for the purpose of the realization of his self which is individual and social at the same time. The eternal problem of human society is the creation of an equilibrium between liberty and social order.

We have now briefly covered some of the major issues concerning the nature and function of the state and the conduct of rule which would be of some help in assessing 'Ali's thoughts on the subject both as fundamental principles and in practice. It must be kept in mind that 'Ali is neither a political philosopher nor a political scientist in the sense in which these terms are generally used. He is first and foremost a religious teacher and therefore his thoughts rotate around and emerge from the fundamental concepts of religious ethics and morality which, indeed, in the case of Islam encompass all aspects of human life—spiritual, social, economic as well as political as an integrated totality. However, before we make some observations on the document, a brief introduction to 'Ali's personality would be in order.

Notes and References
Chapter One

1. See The Qur'an, 2:231; 27:19; 38:26,36; respectively.

2. The Qur'an, 2:129,151 and passim.

3. The term *salih* is so frequently used in the Qur'an along with faith (*iman*), derived from the root *salaha*, is much more comprehensive than it is generally translated. It denotes, good, right, proper, in order, useful, befitting, suitable and appropriate and not only 'righteous' as it is usually translated. See Lane, *Arabic-English Lexicon*, Beirut, 1968, pp 1417 f.

4. W. Montgomery Watt, *Islamic Political Thought*, Edinburgh, 1968, p. 26.

5. Emile Durkheim, *Elementary Forms of the Religious Life*, London, Allen &Unwin, 1915, pp. 416 ff.

6. cf. Morris Ginsberg. *On the Diversity of Morals*, London, Hein-

mann, 1958, p. 231.

7. Seyyed Hossein Nasr, *Islamic Studies*, Librairie Du Liban, Beirut, 1967, p. 6.

8. Fazlur Rahman, *Islam*, Weidenfeld and Nicolson, 1966, p. 12.

9. Abd al-Rahman Ibn Khaldun, *Al-Muqaddima*, Cairo, 1322 AH. p.77; Charles Issawi, *An Arab Philosophy of history: Selection from the Prolegomena of Ibn Khaldun*, London, 1950, p. 99.

10. Ibn Hisham, *Sirat Rasul Allah*, ed. Mustafa Saqqa et. al., Cairo, 1936, vol. ii, pp. 147-150.

11. *Ibid.*

12. *Ibid.*

13. It should be noted that not all of the 52 clauses were written at one time. It appears that after basic terms of the agreement the remaining articles were added at different times when a clan entered into the treaty and thus the whole document took about two years to be completed. See Montgomery Watt, *Muhammad At Medina*, London, 1956. pp. 226f, who made a good analysis of the date of the agreement.

14. Ibn Hisham, loc. cit.

15. R. A. Nicholson, *A Literary History of the Arabs*, Cambridge At the University Press, 1956, p. 173.

16. The account of Saqifa is recorded by almost every historian and hardly needs any particular reference. However, the earliest account is given by Ibn Ishaq, d.768 A.D. (151 A.H.), see Ibn Hishan, op. cit, pp. 306-10.

17. This account can be found in any early history such as Yaqubi, Dinawari, Masudi, etc. We will give specific references only from Muhammad b. Jarir al-Tabari, *Tarikh al-Rusul wa'l-muluk*, ed. M.J. De Goeje, et al; Lieden, 1879-1901, see vol. 1, pp. 2137ff.

18. Tabari, op. cit vol. 1, pp. 2778ff.

19. Tabari, op. cit vol. 1, pp. 2988f and 3066ff.

20. Tabari, op. cit vol. 1, pp 3086f.

21. Abu'l Hasan 'Ali b.Muhammad al-Mawardi, *Al-ahkam al-sultaniyya wa'l wilayat al-diniyya*, Cairo, 1960, pp of.

22. This is one of the points of Islamic law which is accepted by all schools of law and by the Jurists of all times.

23. *Encyclopaedia of Religion and Ethics*, Art. 'Theocracy'.

24. *The Shorter Oxford English Dictionary on Historical Principles*. 'Theocracy'.

25. *Encyclopaedia of Religion and Ethics*, loc. cit.

26. Asghar Ali Engineer, *The Islamic State*, Vikas Publishing House, Bombay 1994, p. 34.

27. Jullundhri, Rashid Ahmad, *Islam And Current Issues*, Institute of Islamic Culture, Lahore, 1997, p. 91; also see Shah Wali Allah, Fiqh Umar translation *Risala Dar Madhhab* Faruq Azam, Abu Yahya Imam Khan Noshahri, Institute of Islamic Culture, Lahore, 1952. Passim.

28. Qamaruddin Khan, *Political Concepts in the Qur'an*, Islamic Book Foundation, Karachi, 1982, p. 44.

29. Sir Muhammad Iqbal, *The Reconstruction of Religious Thought in Islam*, ed. M. Saeed Sheikh, Lahore, 1986, p. 66.

30. Iqbal, op. cit, p. 68.

31. Iqbal, op. cit, p. 10.

32. *The New Encyclopedia Britannica*, Vol. IX, 15th ed. 1980, p. 19.

33. *The Encyclopedia of Modern Islamic World*, New York, Oxford University Press, 1995, Vol. iv, p. 20, cf. Barkes Niyazi, *The Development of Secularism in Turkey*, Montreal, 1964. p. 5.

34. *The Encyclopedia of Modern Islamic World*, loc. cit. cf. E.G. Hobsbawm, *The Age of Revolution*, 1789-1948, New York, 1962, p. 272; Peter E. Glasner, *The Sociology of Religion: A critique of a concept*, London, 1977, p. 115.

35. Mushirul Haque, "Islam in secular India" in John Donohue, ed. *Islam in Transition*, New York, 1982, p. 177.

36. Iqbal op. cit, p. 122.

37. Boulding, K.E., "the concept of social justice", in R.B. Brand, ed. *Social Justice*, Englewood Cliffs, N.Y. 1962, p.3.

38. Cf. Gregory Ulastos, "Justice and Equality", in R.B. Brand, ed. *Social Justice*, op. cit, p.31.

39. Ibn Khaldun, op. cit. p.71.

"I am the city of knowledge and 'Ali is its gate."

(The Prophet -pbuh)

CHAPTER TWO

'Ali bin Abi Talib

The fourth and the last of the *Rashidun* Caliphs, the first Shi'ite Imam, cousin and son-in-law of the Prophet and one who embraced Islam at an early age; ten, at the most thirteen.[1] Adopted by the Prophet in his childhood, Ali grew up under the personal care and guardianship of the recipient of Divine Revelation–the Founder of Islam. These circumstances gave him a unique[2] authority to speak for Islam, its beliefs, its thoughts and fundamental concepts, its theories and practices, its principles and ideals and to interpret the Qur'an and the *Sunna* in all cases of conscience. He is universally recognized for his sagacity, wisdom and profound knowledge of the Qur'an and the *Sunna* of the Prophet. No less a person than the second caliph, 'Umar b. al-Khattab is reported to have said that "'Ali is the best of all judges of the people of al-Medina and the chief of the readers of Qur'an" and that: "let no one give a legal decision when 'Ali is present."[3] Similarly, in later generations, the famous theologian al-Hasan al-Basri called him "the scholar of God in this community" and the great traditionist and jurist Ahmad b. Hanbal, declared that "there has not come down to us regarding the merits of any one of the Companions of the Prophet of God what has been transmitted concerning Ali."[4] This trend of describing 'Ali's personality remains unchanged throughout Islamic literature; and if the criterion of *tawatur*,[5] universally adopted by the Muslim scholars of *hadith* in describing the authenticity of traditions and in other branches of Islamic learning is to be applied to the personal qualities which have been ascribed to 'Ali, there is no reason to doubt the veracity of these reports.

It is, however, not intended, nor indeed is it possible, in this brief introduction to discuss in any detail 'Ali's personality: a combination of the qualities of a brave and chivalrous warrior, a selfless and staunch supporter of the Prophet and Islam, a ruler who never compromised his principles, indeed an embodiment of the Qur'anic ideals of morality and the *sunnah* of the Prophet. He has unanimously been credited with having a philosophical disposition and acclaimed as an unequalled man of letters in the early days of Islam. His numerous speeches, orations, letters and maxims recorded by Muslim historians and biographers from the earliest times bear testimony to the fact that he had no peer in literary accomplishment among the early Muslims. This quality found its best expression when he was called upon by the community to take up the responsibility of the Caliphate in the year 656 A.D. (36 A.H.), after the murder of the third caliph, 'Uthman b. 'Affan. It is in this short period of less than five years; full of turmoil, dissension, unrest, civil strife and indeed of insurmountable difficulties and problems caused by the events which had taken place during the preceding regime and the subsequent murder of 'Uthman, that we come to know 'Ali as the greatest orator Islam has ever produced and the greatest exponent of political thought and principles of administration and conduct of rule, never before so vividly explained. It is in this period that besides giving many speeches and public addresses, he also wrote numerous letters containing his concepts of state and his instructions and advice to his governors and provincial functionaries; 79 of these, scattered in various early sources were collected by al-Sharif al-Radi (d. 405 A.H./1014 A.D.) in the famous collection known as the *Nahj al-Balagha*. These letters, if combined together, would make a gospel of political science and an administrative code for political scientists the world over.

In the society of 7th century Arabia when the people were interested only in the immediate, the particular and the concrete, 'Ali with his profound knowledge of the Qur'an expounded both the sense of the universal underlying particulars and a view of history as a process towards the achievement of greater harmony and better human relationships irrespective of race, religion, color or geographical boundaries. By pondering upon 'Ali's dicta, a political scientist and administrative theorist of the 21st century would be astonished to find an Arab of the 7th century discussing state policies in the light of history as a process of selection and elimination in which the morally unfit are destroyed and replaced by spiritually advanced people. This should not be surprising however. It is now an accepted fact that Islam effected an all-out transformation in 7th century Arabian society. The changes it introduced in institutional life and in social and economic systems were nothing less than a revolution. But perhaps the main triumph of Islam lay in producing a new intellectual and spiritual outlook among the backward people to whom it was first addressed.

The Arabs were not a speculative race like the Greeks. They had little taste for abstract thinking and were interested only in the practical affairs of everyday life. It was the Qur'an, with its concepts of God, man, the universe and their relationship with each other that pushed the Arabs beyond the particular to a grasp of the universal and towards understanding of a universe governed by an impersonal law. It showed the way towards the fundamental truths of life relating the world to God; the body to spirit; the particular to the universal; the individual to society without destroying the distinctive value of any component. Thus, the Qur'an made the Arabs look at life from a philosophical point of view based on the concept of God who is not to be identified with any natural or human phenomenon. The Qur'an, in brief, gave them the rudiments of metaphysics and sociology, as well as an embryonic legal theory. Further, the Qur'an emphatically and repeatedly asserts that the rise and fall of nations is due primarily to the changes in the belief and character of nations. According to the Qur'an, no real revolution occurs in the life of a people until a revolution occurs in their mental and moral outlook: "*Allah does not change the condition of a people until they change their own condition.*"[6]

It was because of this Qur'anic philosophy that for 'Ali, political success at the expense of principles and noble ideals was something inconceivable. His biographers, possessing all shades of opinions have never denied the fact that even the most adverse circumstances he was confronted with during his short-lived Caliphate could not make him budge from his policy and swerve from a high moral standard or to adopt measures of dubious legality to thwart his adversaries. He met with rebellion and machinations from his Syrian challenger.[7] This weakened his position, but he remained as firm and as uncompromising as ever, not yielding to any external pressures or exigencies of time. He was not prepared to sacrifice his noble ideals for the sake of petty, mundane advantages. On the other hand, he strove constantly and unremittingly with all his powers of eloquence, of which he had an abundant share, to convince the people of the soundness of his principles.

In short, the cornerstone of 'Ali's policy was to create a morally good and just society, composed of religiously righteous men with a keen and vivid awareness of God, who enjoins good and forbids evil. Indeed, for a Muslim 'Ali's state and administrative policies are a faithful elaboration on and application of the teachings of the Qur'an and the *Sunna* of the Prophet. Yet a non-Muslim or even a secularist will find in them universally applicable principles of humanitarianism, egalitarianism, social justice, economic justice and a sound basis for a harmonious relationship among men of widely different orientations. He was a zealous champion of equality and justice for all of his subjects, Muslim and non-Muslim alike. To him then, the privileged and the deprived, the strong and the weak, the poor and the rich, the haves and the have-nots are all to be treated with equality and justice.

It would be projection to read modern systems of democracy or socialism in 7th century Arabian polity. Both of these systems in their present form derive from the movements of the Renaissance, Reformation, Enlightenment and the French Revolution. Yet some of the basic concepts of these systems may be found in Ali's political thoughts in rudimentary form. Democracy as it is practiced today is based on eight fundamental concepts: i) rational empiricism; ii) an emphasis on the individual; iii) the instrumental nature of the state; iv) voluntarism; v) the law behind the law; vi) an emphasis on means; vii) discussion and consent in relations; and viii) the basic equality of human beings.[8] On the other hand, the founding principles of socialism are: to create more opportunities for the underprivileged classes; to end inequality based on birth rather than service; to open the horizons of education to all people; to eliminate discriminatory practices based on sex, religion, race, or social class; to regulate and reorganize the economy for the benefit of the whole community; to maintain full employment; to provide adequate social security for the sick, unemployed and aged; to re-plan the layout of towns and cities; to tear down slums and build new housing; to provide medical facilities for everyone, irrespective of thier financial position; and finally, to rebuild society on the foundation of cooperation in lieu of competition, financial incentive and profit.[9] A diligent reader of 'Ali's thoughts would not fail to recognize that some of these ideas of these modern political philosophies were introduced by 'Ali during his caliphate, as far as they were practically possible in 7th century society and under his particular circumstances. Unfortunately, Muslims failed to develop or institutionalize these concepts while the West not only theoretically developed these ideals to their full maturity but also put them into practice.

The first document we present here is the most comprehensive of all the letters of instruction 'Ali wrote to his governors during his Caliphate. It deals with almost every aspect of administration and state, explaining the function and *raison d'etre* of the Islamic State and the duties and obligations of those in terms of their authority and their responsibilities both in relation to the state and the people. It is a code to establish a kind and benevolent rule, throwing light on various aspects of justice, benevolence and mercy; an order based on the ethics of a benign and pious rulership, where justice and mercy are shown to human beings irrespective of class, creed and color, where poverty is neither a stigma nor a disqualification and one where justice is not tarred with nepotism, favoritism, regionalism or religious fanaticism. A social scientist of today would be astonished to read 'Ali's analysis of the various social classes and how to look after each one of them; and that this is as true in 21st century sopciety as it was in the 7th; and it is also equally applicable to any society. One would also be amazed to read that the modern (if it is modern) concept of a welfare state finds its first expression in 'Ali's epistle to his governor.

In reading the document, however, one must keep in mind the extremely trying circumstances which 'Ali faced as he led the community and the state, adhering uncompromisingly to his moral principles, as against the chicanery and duplicity used by his opponent in Syria to wrest the Caliphate from him,[10] a situation never encountered by his three predecessors. When all of these reactionary and conservative forces united together to work against the new Islamic order, 'Ali stood firm in his commitment to reestablishing the Islamic values of simplicity, equality and socio-economic justice, his own sufferings notwithstanding. As no thesis can be understood without comparing it with its antithesis, 'Ali's ideals and principles regarding politics and state cannot be fully grasped unless one takes into consideration the policies adopted by his adversaries. Thus though this document, keeping in view the political situation of the time, one sees that 'Ali changed the concepts of failure and success. To him, success is adherence to noble ideals and principles; failure is to sacrifice them for political and worldly gain.

Before closing this brief introduction, a word about Malik b. al-Harith al-Ashtar al-Nakha'i, to whom the letter is addressed, is appropriate. He came from the tribe of Nakh'a and was one of the prominent *Tabi'un*. He was an extremely brave warrior and took active part in the expeditions dispatched by the Caliph Abu Bakr against the apostate Arabian tribes, proving himself a great champion of Islam against apostasy (*Ridda*).[11] His nickname al-Ashtar is derived from the Arabic root *shatara* which means to cut off or tear off and was given to him when in battle against the apostate tribe of Banu Hanif in 632-33 A.D. (11 A.H.). He fought against one of the most famous and chivalrous Arab warriors Abu Masika al-Iyadi, cutting him in two.

Malik became one of the closest pupils, companions and supporters of 'Ali and fought for him in the battles of al-Jamal (36 A.H./656 A.D.) and Siffin[12] (37 A.H./657 A.D.). He remained one of the trusted followers of 'Ali even in the most adverse circumstances. 'Ali had specially educated him in the principles of administration and jurisprudence. When Muhammad b. Abi Bakr, the stepson (*al-rabib*) of Ali and his governor in Egypt, was killed in 658 A.D. (38 A.H.), by 'Amr b. al-'As, whom Mu'awiya had sent with an army of 400, 'Ali appointed Malik al-Ashtar as the new governor of that turbulent province. It was on this occasion that 'Ali wrote this historic document for his disciple-governor designate.

When the news of Malik's appointment reached 'Amr b. al-'As, he was alarmed because of the former's bravery, courage and great skill in warfare for which he was well known. Malik did not reach al-Fustat, the then capital of Egypt, as he was poisoned by a drink of honey offered to him at al-'Arish,[13] only a few miles from al-Fustat by a *dihqan* in the pay of 'Amr.[14] Consequently Egypt was lost to 'Ali and passed into the hands of Mu'awiya

Notes and References
Chapter Two

1. 'Ali's age is variously reported as ranging from ten to thirteen years at the time when Muhammad received his first revelation. According to Ibn Ishaq and a majority of the early sources, he was only ten years old at the time. See Ibn Hisham, *Sirat Rasul Allah*, ed. Mustafa Saqqa, et al, Cairo 1936, i:262; al-Baladhuri, *Ansab al-Ashraf*, ed. Muhammad Hamidullah, Cairo 1955, i: 112; Ibn Sa'd, *al-Tabaqat al-Kubra*, Beirut 1957, iii, pp. 2If. Also see a fuller discussion as to who was the first male to accept Islam and of his age at the time in Ibn 'Abd al-Barr, *al-Isti'ab*, Cairo n.d., v. iii, p. 109 ff., Ibn Hajar, *Tahzib al-Tahzib*, Hyderabad 1326 A.H., v. iii, p. 336.

2. See for example, the tradition recorded by Ahmad b. Hanbal given below.

3. Ibn Sa'd, op. cit., v. ii, pp. 338 ff; Ibn Abi'l-Hadid, *Sharh Nahj al-Balagha*, ed. Muhammad Abu 'l Fadl Ibrahim, Cairo 1965, v. i, p. 18.

4. *Musnad*, Cairo 1895, v. i, pp. 108, 114 and 118.

5. *Tawatur* is a technical term used especially in the science of *Hadith* to indicate a communication handed down on many sides and which has been well known from very early times. It needs hardly be pointed out that the techniques adopted by the

traditionists such as al-Bukhari and others were used not only by the historians but indeed by scholars in all other branches of learning in Islam.

6. The Qur'an, 13:11.

7. See footnote 10 below.

8. W. Ebemstein, *Today's Isms*, Englewood Cliffs, N.J. 4th edition, 1964, p. 133.

9. *Ibid*, p. 203.

10. Muslim historians and writers from the earliest times until to-day have reported these facts in great detail. See an admirable discussion on these events by Abu'l A'la Mawdudi, *Khilafat wa Mulukiyat*, (in Urdu), Lahore 1966, where he cites many original sources with his own comments.

11. Ibn Sa'd, vi, p. 213; Ibn Hajr, *Tahdhib*, x, p. 12.

12. Ibn Hajr, loc. cit.

13. Al-Arish, one of the oldest Mediterranean coastal towns of the ancient Roman Empire, was known as Laris in the first century A.D. Situated in a fertile oasis surrounded by sand on the frontier between Palestine and Egypt, it became one of the largest cities of pre-lslamic Egypt. When it was named al-'Arish is not quite clear from the sources; it may be before the Arab conquest of Egypt because of the dominant Arab population in that region. It contained a great market and many inns and merchants had their agents there. It seems that the town had long been of a considerable importance as it was the first Egyptian town captured by 'Amr b. al-'As in 640 A.D. (19 A.H.) with the help of 15000 troops; in 1799 it was occupied by Napoleon and the following year, a treaty was concluded in the town, by which the

French were forced to evacuate Egypt. The town still exists with the same name. Yaqut, *Mu'jam al-Buldan* ed. Wustenfeld, Leipzig, 1868, v. iii, p. 660: also see El2 article "Al-'Arish"; Sir William Muir, *The Caliphate: Its Rise, Decline and Fall*, Beirut 1963, p. 170.

14. Mas'udi, *Muruj al-Dhahab*, Beirut 1965, v. ii, p. 409; Ibn 'Imad, *Shadharat al-Dhahab*, Cairo, 1350 AH, v. 1, p. 33; al-Yafi'i, *Mirat al-Jinan*, Beirut 1970, v. i, p. 106.

"'Ali's discourses preserved for us in the famous collection entitled Nahj al-Balagha *are the most authentic and eloquent interpretations of the Qur'an and the Sunna of the Prophet (pbuh). It also bears testimony to the fact that 'Ali had no peer in literary accomplishment among the early Muslims."*

(Shaykh Muhammad Abduh)

CHAPTER THREE

The Nahj al-Balagha

Our main source for these documents is the famous collection comprising 'Ali's speeches, letters and maxims known as the *Nahj al-Balagha*, compiled by Muhammad b. al-Husayn al-Sharif al-Radi (d. 405 A.H./1014 A.D.). Some scholars have expressed doubt about the authenticity of the *Nahj al-Balagha*, suggesting that al-Sharif al-Radi himself composed most of its material and attributed it to 'Ali. Extensive research has been carried out and published on this subject, especially in the last few decades, with these allegations found to be totally baseless. Imtiyaz 'Ali 'Arshi, a distinguished Indian scholar, in his excellent article "Istinad-Nahj al-Balagha,"[1] first published in 1954, was able to trace a considerable part of it in works written long before al-Sharif al-Radi. Following the same line of investigation, I made further research into the subject and discovered all of the material which appears in the *Nahj al-Balagha* in works compiled long before the time of al-Sharif.[2] These sources include Ibrahim al-Thaqafi's (d. 283 A.H./896 A.D.) *Kitab al-Gharat* (Teheran nd.); Nasr b. Muzahim's (d. 212 A.H./827 A.D.) *Waq'at Siffin*, (Cairo 1382 A.H./1962 A.D.); Ya'qubi's (d. 284 A.H./897 A.D.) *Ta'rikh* (Beirut 1379 A.H./1960 A.D.); al-Jahiz's (d. 255 A.H./868 A.D.) *al-Bayan wa'l-Tabyin* (Cairo 1965); Al-Baladhuri's (d. 279 A.H./982-93 A.D.) *Ansab al-Ashraf* (Jerusalem and Cairo 1956 ff.); al-Mubarrad's (d. 285 A.H./898 A.D.) *al-Kamil* (Cairo nd.); al-Tabari's (d. 311 A.H./923 A.D.) *Ta'rikh al-Rusul wa'l-Muluk* (Leiden 1879-1901); and many other well-known works of the second, third and fourth centuries, whereas al-Sharif al-Radi died in the early fifth century. However, we will for now examine only the sources of those documents which we are presenting here in English translation.

The evidence leaves no doubt of 'Ali's authorship. Internally, they contain no such doctrinal or polemical points which may be used in favor of one group of Muslims against another and therefore, there is no reason to suspect any forgery or falsification on the part of al-Sharif or any of the Shi'ites before him. Secondly, all of the ideas expressed in these documents can easily be traced to and compared with the teachings of the Qur'an and the *Sunnah* of the Prophet, which 'Ali had fully absorbed and with his own great intellectual capabilities and religious fervor, had explained for the guidance of the community and the Muslim state. Other internal evidence derived from the vocabulary and style can also be put forward, but we would avoid these for the sake of brevity.

As for the external evidence, the documents or their references can be located in works written before the *Nahj al-Balagha* and can also be found in works written after al-Sharif but evidently using authorities and sources other than those used by him, as we shall see below. As for the first document, its references can be found in the following sources before and after al-Sharif.

1. Abu Muhammad al-Hasan b. 'Ali b. Shu'ba (d. ca. 332 A.H./943 A.D.) gives complete text of the document in his book *Tuhafal-Uqul*.[3] Ibn Shu'ba is regarded as one of the most eminent theologians and traditionalists of the Shi'is of the 3rd–4th centuries.

2. Abu Hanifa Nu'man b. Muhammad, commonly known as al-Qadi Nu'man, a great jurist, traditionist, theologian and historian of the Fatimid dynasty of Egypt (d. 363 A.H./973 A.D.) in his famous work *Da'a'im al-Islam*[4] records the document in full. It is not possible to discuss here in any detail the importance of al-Qadi Nu'man in the literary history of Islam, Arabic literature in general and in Isma'ili literature in particular. Suffice it to say that he was not only the chief historian and theologian but also the chief exponent of the Isma'ili School of Jurisprudence. Thus being the official Jurist and chief judge of the Fatimid Caliphs he deemed this historical document of instruction as the best model for rulers to follow.

3. Shihab al-din Ahmad b. Abd al-Wahhab al-Nuwayri, (d. 732 A.H./1331 A.D.), in his *Nihayat al-Arab fi Funun AlAdab*,[5] also preserves this document. Though al-Nuwayri wrote much later, the importance of his work can hardly be overstated, enjoying the status of a classic

of Arabic literature. His selection of the document in a purely literary work, especially his introductory note in its praise and appreciation is therefore most significant for our purpose. Commenting on the document al-Nuwayri remarks:

> "No bequest from any king or ruler which has come down to us has ever been so rich in meaning and purposefulness, and so comprehensive and universal in applicability as that which 'Ali b. Abi Talib wrote for Malik b. al-Harith al-Ashtar when he appointed him his governor of Egypt. Even though it is a very lengthy one I would prefer to record it in full, because of the fact that such a bequest cannot be left out or omitted, and that no one should remain ignorant of its excellence (*fadl*)."[6]

One very important point to be noted here is that the document as recorded by these four writers including al-Sharif al-Radi has many variants and differences in reading. In Ibn Shu'ba's recension, there are quite a number of words and even phrases which are not found in the *Nahj al-Balagha*. Similarly, there are serious textual variants in Qadi Nu'man's recension from both his predecessor Ibn Shu'ba and his successor, al-Sharif al-Radi. Had the Sharif copied the document from Ibn Shu'ba, who compiled his work at least half a century prior to the *Nahj al-Balagha*, or from al-Qadi Nu'man who wrote his *Da'a'im al-Islam* about 30 years before the *Nahj al-Balagha*, then there should have not been so many variants in the text of the *Tuhaf*, *Da'a'im al-Islam* and *Nahj al-Balagha*. Likewise the text of al-Nuwayri, who wrote about two centuries after the Sharif, considerably differs from all three sources discussed above. This makes it obvious that Ibn Shu'ba, al-Qadi Nu'man, al-Radi and al-Nuwayri received or copied the document from different sources and authorities, independently of each other. This in fact speaks strongly in favour of the authenticity of the document, suggesting that it must have been in wide circulation and copied by various writers and scribes over time. Variants in reading in the oft-repeated traditions are, however, unavoidable.

4. Ahmad b. 'Ali b. Ahmad b. al-'Abbas al-Najashi (b.372/982, d.

450/1058) in his *Kitab al-Rijal*, refers to the document in his biography of Asbagh b. Nubata and says: "He was one of the closest companions of Ali and lived long enough after him and transmitted 'Ali's bequest to Malik al-Ashtar and also 'Ali's bequest to his son Muhammad b. al-Hanafiy".[7] Since al-Najashi deals with the biographical data of the early personalities with only references to the works or traditions handed down by them, he is not expected to record the text of the document. He however does give the complete chain of those through whom the document had been transmitted as follows:

> Ibn al-Jundi from 'Ali b. Hamam from Himyari from Harun b. Muslim from Husayn b. 'Ulwan from Sa'd b. Tarif from Asbagh b. Nubata.[8]

5. Abu Ja'far Muhammad b. al-Hasan b. 'Ali al-Tusi, known as al-Shaykh al-Ta'ifa al-Imamiya or al-Shaykh al-Tusi (b. 385/995 d. 460/1067), in his *al-Fihrist*, also describes the document in the biography of Asbagh b. Nubata.[9] Al-Tusi's biographical notice of Asbagh is almost the same as that of al-Najashi, but his chain of transmitters varies somewhat, reading:

> Ibn Abi Jayyid informed us from Muhammad b. al-Hasan from Himyari from Harun b. Muslim and al-Hasan b. Tarif, all of them from Husayn b. 'Ulwan al-Kulayni from Sa'd b. Tarif from Asbagh b. Nubata.[10]

It may be useful to note in passing that both al-Najashi and al-Tusi were the younger contemporaries of al-Sharif al-Radi; al-Najashi being thirteen years older than al-Tusi, but both old enough to have met the Sharif, probably at the time that he was engaged in compiling the *Nahj al-Balagha*.

6. Ibn 'Asakir, (b. 499 A.H./1105 A.D., d. 571 A.H./1176 A.D.) in his valuable work *Ta'rikh Madinat Dimashq*,[11] in referring to the document gives almost the same *isnad* as those of al-Najashi and al-Tusi, with the difference that Ibn 'Asakir's chain of transmitters goes back to

Muhajir b. 'Umayr.[12] These three *isnad*, very close to each other, from three different sources of great importance leads us to believe that the document has been transmitted through reliable channels.

7. Finally, mention must be made of Ibn Abi'l Hadid (d. 656 A.H./1258 A.D.) who wrote a voluminous commentary[13] on the *Nahj al-Balagha*. Ibn Tiqtaqa tells us that Ibn Abi'l Hadid had an encyclopedic knowledge possessed by very few persons in Islam. He had ten thousand rare books and manuscripts in his personal library.[14] His commentary on the *Nahj al-Balagha* is also an invaluable source of early Islamic history as some of the early treatises used in this work are not to be found even in al-Tabari, though these treatises are referred to by Ibn Nadim, al-Najashi, al-Tusi, and other bibliographers. Ibn Abi'l-Hadid's death occurred in the year of Hulagu's invasion of Baghdad (1258 A.D.), and his personal library, as indeed the entire city with all its precious treasures and libraries was destroyed when Baghdad was plundered and burned by the Mongol hordes. Had the rich libraries of Baghdad not been destroyed, as Imtiyaz 'Ali 'Arshi observes, we would have been able to locate every word of the *Nahj al-Balagha* in the earlier sources.[15] However, Ibn Abi'l Hadid, after giving a detailed commentary on the document which runs to 77 pages (pp. 53-103) discusses at length its importance in Islamic political and administrative thought. After every major point in the document, he writes page after page to show how it is echoed in the advice tendered to Muslim kings and rulers by their advisers and explains how it influenced the pious Umayyad Caliph 'Umar b. 'Abd al-'Aziz. At the end he compares in great detail (pp. 118-130) this document with a number of administrative codes and many a bequest made by kings and caliphs both before and after Islam. He then concludes, saying:

"None can reach the wisdom and sagacity of 'Ali expressed in his bequest to Malik al-Ashtar."[16]

Notes and References
Chapter Three

1. "Faran"; Karachi, May 1954; Arabic translation in *Thaqafat al-Hind*, Delhi, India, December 1957; and most recently, a revised edition in book form, Lucknow, 1972.

2. We have enough evidence that numerous scholars of the first, second and third centuries after the Hijra compiled 'Ali's discourses, but most of these did not survive. Moreover, after the appearance of the *Nahj al-Balagha*; Its excellence in many ways eclipsed that of the earlier works, many of which were lost over the course of time.

3. Ed. Muhammad Sadiq, 5th edition, Iran, 1394 A.H., pp. 83-99.

4. Ed. A.A.A. Fyzee, Cairo 1951-61, v. i, pp. 350-368.

5. Cairo 1935, vol. vi, pp. 19-32.

6. Al-Nuwayri, *Nihayat*, vi, p. 19.

7. Al-Najashi, *Rijal*, p. 7. For the significance of al-Najashi's *Rijal*, see E.G. Brown's valuable discussion of biographical authorities in his *A Literary History of Persia*, vol. iv, pp. 355-58.

8. Al-Najashi, loc. cit.

9. Al-Tusi, *al-Fihrist*, ed. Mahmud Ramyar, Mashhad University Press, (Azarmah 1351), p. 62f. On the importance of al-Tusi's *al-Fihrist*. see Sprenger's preface to his *Bibliotheca Indica*, Calcutta 1853, and Brown, loc. cit.

10. Al-Tusi, loc. cit.

11. Al-Zahiriya Library MS. vol. xii: fol. 119f.

12. Ibn Hajr, *Tahdhib* vol. x, p. 223.

13. Latest edition in 20 volumes ed. by Muhammad Abu'l Fadl Ibrahim, Cairo 1965.

14. *Al-fakhri fi'l adab al-Sultaniya*, Cairo 1921, p. 295.

15. 'Arshi, *Istinad*, p. 46.

16. *Sharh*, vol. xvii, p. 130.

Section Two

The Conduct of Rule in Islam

*"O you who believe, stand out firmly for justice as witnesses
for God, even though it be against yourselves, or
your parents, or your relatives, and whether it be (against)
a rich or a poor man, for God can best protect both.
So follow not the lusts (of your hearts), lest you swerve,
and if you distort (justice), verily God is well-acquainted
with all you do."*

(*The Qur'an, 4:135*)

50

CHAPTER FOUR

'Ali's Letter to his Governor in Egypt

Introductory note by Shan

> From another letter[1] which Ali (peace be upon him!) wrote to Malik b. al-Harith (b. 'Abd Yaghuth) al-Ashtar al-Nakha'i when he appointed him governor of Egypt and its dependencies after the rule of the previous governor, Muhammad b. Abi Bakr was violently disturbed.[2] This is 'Ali's longest bequest[3] (letter of appointment) and the most comprehensive of all of his letters in its excellence and beauty.

"In the name of God, the Merciful, the Compassionate. This is what the slave of God, 'Ali, the commander of the Faithful ordered Malik bin al-Harith al-Ashtar in his bequest (instrument of instructions) to him when he ('Ali) appointed him governor of Egypt, charging him to collect its revenue, to fight its enemies,[4] to ameliorate the lot of its inhabitants and to populate its cities.

'Ali orders al-Ashtar to fear God, to prefer (over every thing else) obedience to Him, to follow what He has commanded in His Book: His compulsory injunctions and His approved way of conduct and behavior,[5] for no one can be happy without following them and no one will be miserable except by denying and neglecting them. And ('Ali orders al-Ashtar) to help God, the Glorious, with his heart, his hand and his tongue;[6] for He, the Exalted, has undertaken to help those who help Him and to honor those who honor Him.[7]

'Ali further orders him to curb his self (*nafs*) in the face of carnal desires and to restrain it when it (*self*) shows signs of refractoriness, for verily the human *self* is a great prompter to evil except if God is merciful to one.

Then know, O Malik! that I am sending you (as governor) to a country over which there have passed before your time several periods of justice and injustice (i.e. dynasties of just and unjust rulers). The people there will watch your doings as you watch the doings of the governors before you and will say about you what you say about them. Remember that the virtuous can only be pointed out (i.e. recognized) by what God makes to pass on the tongues of His slaves (i.e. people); and so let the dearest treasure to you be the treasure of virtuous acts. Control therefore your desires and appetites and be niggardly to yourself in what is unlawful to you, for such niggardliness towards one's self is to do justice to it concerning what it likes or dislikes.[8]

Let your heart be imbued with mercy for your subjects as well as love and kindness for them. You must not be like a fierce beast which wishes to devour them. For your subjects are of two categories: either a brother of yours in faith, or similar to you in build (i.e. human be-ings like you[9]). Both of them make many mistakes and are subject to many defects. They do commit certain mistakes either intentionally or unintentionally. Extend to them (all) your forgiveness and pardon, just as you would wish God to grant you His forgiveness and pardon; for you are above them and he who has appointed you governor is above you, while God is above him who has appointed you; and indeed, God expects you to manage their affairs efficiently and through them He will test you.

You must never expose yourself to a conflict with God,[10] for you have no strength to ward off His punishment and cannot do without His pardon and mercy. Do not repent for having forgiven anyone, nor rejoice over any punishment that you may mete out to anyone. Do not hasten towards a rash act from which you could find an escape[11] and never say, "I am your overlord (because) I order and am obeyed," for such ideas corrupt the heart and weaken faith, bringing one to misfor-tune.

And when the power you enjoy produces vanity and arrogance in your mind, look at the greatness of the kingdom of God above you and His power in respect to you of doing what you are unable to do in respect to yourself; for such a thought would help to curb your ambition and would check your sharpness (*gharb*)[12] bringing back to you the part of your intellect which has gone astray.

Beware of competing with God in His greatness and in trying to resemble Him in His might, for God humiliates every tyrant or oppressor and disgraces every braggart.

Be just to God[13] in respect to yourself as well as to other men; and also in respect to your close friends and those of your subjects of whom you are fond,[14] for if you do not do this (equity and justice) you will certainly be a tyrant and an oppressor. When a person tyrannizes and oppresses the creatures of God, not only His creatures but God Himself becomes his opponent; and whoever enters into a disputation with God [in His authority or disobeys Him in any way] invalidates his arguments and God remains at war with him until he recants or repents. Nothing invites a change in the kindness of God and His swift retribution more powerfully than persistence in injustice, for God hears the invocations and prayers of the oppressed ones and He is always on the lookout for the oppressors.

The Masses and the Ruler:

Let the dearest of your concerns be the middle course in truth,[15] the most general in justice [in its applicability to every one] and the most comprehensive of popular approval for the approval of the elite is rendered futile by the disapproval of the masses, while the disapproval of the elite is obviated by the approval of the common people.

From among the subjects there is none more burdensome to the governor than the elite in the matter of seeking favors in a state of prosperity and least helpful to him in troublesome times, more hateful of justice, more importunate in making demands, less grateful when given anything, slower in accepting any excuse when their demands are not met and weaker in patience under the calamities of time (i.e. in difficult times they will not be faithful and loyal); while the pillars of the faith, the bulwark of the Muslims and a shield against enemies are the common people of the state. You should therefore lean upon them and show your fondness for them.

Let the farthest of your subjects and the most distant of them from you be the man who most keenly seeks the defects of the people, for surely there are certain defects in the people and the governor is the most appropriate person to overlook them. Do not therefore try to discover such of their defects as are hidden from you, for your duty is to remove those defects which are apparent, while God is to decide about such of them as are concealed from you.[16] Cover the weaknesses of the people as far as you can, so that God may veil those weaknesses of yours which you would like to remain hidden from your subjects.

Remove the cause of every grudge in the hearts of the people and cut off from yourself the links of every vengefulness. Ignore whatever is not clear to you (i.e. of which you are not sure) and do not hastily believe the words of a slanderer or a backbiter, for a backbiter is a fraud, even though he may appear in the guise of a well wisher.

The Counselors and the Ministers:

Do not include in your consultation a miser who may turn you away from generosity and frighten you with poverty; nor [take counsel of] a coward who may weaken your performance in the affairs of state, or a greedy one who may embellish for your avarice with injustice. Indeed, miserliness, cowardice and greed are (only) different characteristics which all go to make up a lack of faith in God.

The worst of your ministers is he who was a minister to the wicked before you and who was a partner in their sinful deeds.[17] Let such men be not your intimate companions,[18] because they are the helpers of sinful persons and the brothers of tyrants. You can find better substitutes for them from among those who have equal ability as far as judgment and sharpness of wit is concerned, but are not laden with burdens of sin like them; [take your ministers] from among those who have never helped a tyrant in his [acts of] tyranny or sinner in his impiety. Such persons would be easier for you to provide (i.e. less encumbrance in maintenance), better qualified to help you, more attentive to you in their friendship and less attached to anyone other than you.

So choose such men for your companionship in private and in public and even among them the most favored[19] of you be the one who tells you the bitter truth most frankly and is the least helpful to you in anything done by you which God dislikes for His friends,[20] however desirable it may appear to you. Attach yourself to the virtuous and the truthful and do not allow them to be to flatter you or admire you falsely for what you have not done; for flattery breeds vanity and brings one close to arrogance and haughtiness.

And let not the virtuous and wicked be equal in your sight, for this would discourage good men from doing good and encourage the wicked in doing evil; impose upon each of them what he has imposed upon himself.

You should know that nothing prompts a good opinion of a ruler among his subjects more powerfully than his kindness to them,[21] his lightening of their burdens and his not forcing them to do anything to which they have not been used. This conduct on your part will join your subjects together in having tender feelings towards you and forming a good opinion of you. Such goodwill (so cultivated by both the ruler and the ruled) will remove from you a [feeling of] constant anxiety.[22] Verily, the man who deserves the most of your confidence and trust is he whom you have treated well; and the man who deserves most to be suspected by you is he whom you have treated badly.

Do not break any virtuous practice which the leaders of this nation had followed, by which mutual love had been secured and due to which the subjects had prospered. Do not create any new practice which may harm any of those old practices, for in that case the reward will be for him who had established them and the onus of having broken any one of them would be on you.

Consult frequently with the scholars and discuss often with the wise men (*hukama'*) matters which may be conducive to the prosperity of your land and which may go to strengthen what had been established by your predecessors.

The Different Classes of the People:

You should remember that the subjects are composed of various classes, each of which cannot prosper without the other and cannot dispense with each other's help. One of these classes is the soldiers of God, another the secretaries dealing either directly with the masses or working for the officials of the state, another the dispensers of justice (judges), another the officials or functionaries (of the department) of justice and redress (i.e. those who enforce and maintain law and order and guard the peace and prosperity of the country), another the collectors of the poll-tax (*jizya*) and land revenue (*kharaj*) from the covenanted people (*dhimmis*) as well as the Muslims, still another the merchants and artisans and lastly, the lowest one consisting of needy and destitute people. God has prescribed for each of them their due share and has fixed their rights and duties in His Book (Qur'an) or in the practice of His Prophet (*sunna*) which is preserved for us.

The armed forces, by the Grace of God, are the fortress of the subjects, the ornaments of the governors, the honor of the faith and the means of securing peace. The state cannot stand without them. The army cannot be maintained without the revenue (collected by the state through tax collectors) which God provides for them from the land. With this they acquire sufficient strength to fight their enemies and on which they depend for their welfare and which satisfies their needs.

Then these two classes (tax-collectors and the military) find their strength only in a third category, consisting of judges, government officials and secretaries, who give decisions about contracts,[23] preserve various interests (of the state and the people, such as revenue, law and order, peace and amity among diverse classes of society and in settling litigation) and are entrusted with [looking after] affairs both general and specialized.

Again, these classes cannot prosper without the traders and artisans who devote themselves to providing comforts to all other sections of society, the traders by establishing their markets (to provide the necessities of life) and the artisans by providing with their hands[24] others with such amenities as no one else can provide. And lastly, there is the lowest class comprising the needy and poor persons who deserve to be helped and assisted. Indeed, God has provided abundant means and scope for all of these classes and each one of them has a claim on the governor for at least what is necessary for its maintenance and well being.

And [remember] that the governor cannot perform properly all the duties that God has imposed upon him except by careful application and sincerely seeking His help, by accustoming himself to stick to what is right and to put up with it patiently, however light or heavy it may be.

The Army and its Organization:

Appoint as commander of your soldiers one who in your opinion is the most sincere of them in his devotion to God, to the Prophet and to your Imam, who is the cleanest of them of character (lit. pocket)[25] and the best of them in gentleness—he who is slow to get angry, is fond of accepting excuses, is kind and compassionate to the weak and stern to the strong, whose displeasure does not goad him to violence and whose calmness does not make him helpless and inactive.

Then stick to those [from among your soldiers] who are possessors of honor and virtue (*muruwwa*)[26] and are descended from noble ancestors (*ahsab*, sing. *Hasab*),[27] belong to virtuous families (*buyutat*, sing. *bayt*)[28] with a record of exalted traditions and meritorious deeds in the past. Similarly stick to those who have magnanimity and are brave and courageous as well as those who are generous and benevolent, for these (persons of such qualities) constitute a group of noble men and a set of virtuous people.

Then look after them as parents look after their children.[29] Let nothing with which you could strengthen and improve their condition appear too much to your mind, nor you should look with contempt[30] on any act of kindness which you may mete out to them, however small it might be; for it would prompt them to offer you their sincerity and loyalty and think well of you. Do not neglect to look after their minor problems by restricting your attention only to the major ones, for even a small favor from you has a place[31] and they can benefit by it just as the major problems have their own occasion and cannot be disposed of without your help.

Let your most preferred of the commanders of your army be the one who treats the soldiers sympathetically and bestows on them from whatever he has at his disposal as much as may satisfy their needs as well as the needs of the members of their families whom they leave behind [when they go to war]. Your kind treatment of the commanders will make their hearts incline towards you (i.e. make them loyal to you).

The real satisfaction and happiness of governors lies in the establishment of justice in their land and the love and affection which the subjects show for them; but (remember) that the subjects' affection does not appear unless their hearts are free from rancor [against the rulers] and that they feel themselves to be safe and secure. Their sincerity [for the rulers] likewise is not ensured unless the rulers keep under watch the officers who manage their affairs so that the people do not think of their rule as a heavy burden (i.e. oppressive) and wish for its termination.

Let then their hopes find full scope in you, praise them continuously and express your appreciation repeatedly for the exploits of those of them who have performed good deeds, for a frequent mention of their noble acts will inspire the brave ones and encourage even the laggard, if God so wills.

Then also appreciate and recognize each man for what he has

achieved and do not ascribe the achievements of any man to someone else. Do not fail to give him full credit for his achievement and let not the high rank of anyone prompt you to magnify a small achievement of his, or the humble status of another man to belittle any of his great achievements.

Refer to God and to His Prophet such of your problems as baffle you or any matter which appears to be doubtful to you, for God has ordered those whom He wants to guide: *"O you who believe, obey God and obey the Prophet as well as those in authority from among you and if you have a dispute about any matter refer it to God and the Prophet."*[32] To refer to God means to follow His Book which is perfect and firm, while referring to the Prophet is to stick to his *Sunna* which is unanimously accepted and about which there is no difference of opinion.

Selection of Judges:

Select for the administration of justice one who in your opinion is the best of your subjects[33]—he who is not impeded by [the complexity of] any situation and is not carried away by anger because of the wrangling of the litigants, who does not persist in [his] error when he recognizes it, whose mind is not prone to avarice and who is not contented with the superficial understanding of a thing;[34] one who deliberates most seriously on every doubtful or ambiguous point, makes the greatest use of arguments and proof, is the least impatient with lengthy and recurring arguments, waits most patiently for events to unfold themselves and is the most decisive and firm when a judgment becomes clear;[35] he who is not misled by flattery or excessive praise and is not won over by enticement; and indeed such people are few.

Once you have selected and appointed such people to act as your judges, then from time to time you should personally examine their work and their decisions. Pay them generously so that their financial worries are completely removed and they may not be in need of [help from] other people. Give them such a prestigious place near you that no one else from among your favorite companions may covet,[36] so that they may be safe from the calumny of other men.[37] Pay utmost attention to all this, because authority or the code of law (*dīn*)[38] has been a prisoner in the hands of wicked persons with which they have only gratified their [personal] desires and sought after worldly gain.[39]

State Officials and Functionaries:

Then look into the matters [regarding the selection] of your officials and appoint them after due testing (of their capabilities and character) and not on the basis of partiality or personal preference, for these two things combine in themselves various kinds of injustice and dishonesty. Choose from among them men of experience and modesty belonging to noble families and possessing a status in early Islam, for they are the noblest in character, most untarnished of honor, the least disposed to greed ends and the most mindful of the consequences of all affairs.

Then allow them ample salaries, for this will help them to improve their condition (i.e. to maintain themselves with honor and dignity) and prevent them from misappropriating what is under their control (i.e. State funds which they hold in their trust); this will also give you a proof[40] against them if they disobey your orders or betray your trust.

Also keep on (confidentially and secretly) investigating their activities, sending out spies who are loyal and trustworthy to watch over them. For your secret observation of their affairs will induce them to behave honestly and to treat their subjects leniently.[41]

And also watch carefully your subordinates; if any of them commits a breach of faith (i.e. is accused of dishonesty) which is reported by more than one person (i.e. confirmed) by your secret service, regard this as sufficient evidence. Then inflict physical punishment on him, holding him responsible for the act committed by him and disgrace him, brand him as a traitor and chastise him with the shame of gross misconduct.

Revenue Administration:

Pay careful attention to the matter of land revenue (i.e. its collection) in such a way as must ensure the welfare of those who pay it, because on the proper arrangement of tax [collection] and the condition of those who pay it depends the welfare of all other [sections of the population]. Nay, the others cannot prosper without their (i.e. tax payers) prosperity. Indeed, the entire population is wholly dependent on the land revenue as well as those who pay it.

But you should give your attention more to the populating and the prosperity of land[42] than the collection of the tax, for the latter cannot be obtained without populating the land and (ensuring) its prosperity. And he who demands the tax without inhabiting and ensuring the flourishing of the land ruins the country, destroys the people and does not rule for long.

If the taxpayers complain of any undue burden, (i.e. heavy taxation) an obstacle or stoppage of irrigation water or rainfall or the deterioration of any land which has been submerged by flood water or stricken by drought, you should grant them such relief as you consider to be conducive to their welfare.

Let not any relief granted to them weigh heavily on your mind for they will repay it to you by populating and your country and making it flourish; beautifying your dominion, while you would at the same time earn their admiration and praise and feel happy at having doled out justice to them. You can also then (safely) rely on the extra strength they have gained due to the respite given by you and they will feel confident of your kindness towards them on account of the just treatment to which they have become accustomed. Then in case something may happen for which you have to depend upon them (i.e. their help), they will bear it willingly (i.e. they will help you wholeheartedly). For a prosperous land can bear the burden you place on it; and the ruination of the land springs from the poverty of its inhabitants; and the inhabitants become impoverished when the rulers hanker after hoarding [wealth] because they are doubtful of their tenure [of office] and derive no benefit from the examples of their predecessors.[43]

Secretaries and Scribes Attached Directly to the Governor:

Carefully examine the integrity of your scribes and secretaries and entrust your work[44] only to those who are the best among them; and assign such of your confidential correspondence (lit. letters) which contain your strategic plans and your secrets [of the State affairs] exclusively to those who combine in themselves all of the noble traits and are not emboldened by their privileged position to misbehave with you in the presence of the common people. Negligence must not make them negligent in placing before you the letters of your officials and sending replies to them with your approval in connection with what they (the official) require from you and what has been granted by you. No pact or treaty which has been entered into on your behalf should be defective or harmful [to the State], nor should they be incapable of solving any problem which has become complicated.[45] They should not be unaware of the extent of their personal value (i.e. their proper place, rank and the responsibilities entailed), for he who is ignorant of his own personal value is still more ignorant of the value of any other man.

Then let not your selection of them (for such important duties) be based merely on your good sense and affection towards them or on your opinion (i.e. personal liking) of them, because men often ingratiate themselves with their rulers by means of showing their affection (lit. hypocrisy) for you and by their pleasant conversation[46] (i.e. flattery), while there is nothing beyond that of sincerity or honesty. And thus you must judge (lit. test) them through their work (i.e. previous record of service) under the virtuous rulers before your time and appoint one who is the best of them in his dealings with the common people and the most reputed for honesty; this will indeed be a proof of your sincerity to God as well as to him who has appointed you to the office of governor.

Appoint for every category of your work (i.e. different administrative branches of the government) a chief from among your officers who may not be nonplussed by any problem or by the large amount of work. Remember that any defect or weakness that there may be in your secretaries which is overlooked by you will be ascribed to you (i.e. you will be held responsible for it).

Trade and Industry:

As far as the merchants and artisans are concerned, you are advised to treat them well and give them good counsel. Some of them stay [in one place] permanently, others move about with their goods from place to place and [the artisans] who earn their livelihood by manual labor all are sources of profit (to the State and country) and the means of life's comforts (i.e. the necessities of life). They procure or import commodities and articles of trade from distant and far-flung places, from land as well as from across the seas, from the plain as well as from the mountains; and from such places as are beyond the reach of common man which he cannot dare approach. These traders are (generally) peace-loving people from whom no mischief should be feared and they are friends not to be dreaded for treachery or disorder.

You must therefore look after their interests whether they are [trading] in your capital or are on the borders of your territory; but remember at the same time that a good many of them are intensely hard bargainers (i.e. charging exorbitant prices) and extremely stingy and greedy for profits, acting arbitrarily in their sales transactions (i.e. by hoarding and monopolizing commodities to command high prices). Such a condition is extremely harmful to the public and a discredit to the ruler. Forbid hoarding, for the Prophet of God, peace be upon him and his family members, has forbidden it. And see to it that trade is carried on with goodwill and generosity and that the scales (measures and weights) are held even with honesty and uprightness and [goods are sold] at such rates which do not harm either the buyer or the seller. He who is found guilty of hoarding after you have prohibited it, inflict upon him appropriate punishment.

The Poor and the Destitute:

Then, O Malik, for God's sake pay special attention to the lower classes consisting of those who have no resources of their own, namely the helpless and the poor, the miserable and the crippled, some of whom beg while others (who maintain self-respect) do not beg. For God's sake protect them (all) with what He has entrusted to you out of His right concerning these people. Spend on (every one of) them a portion of the public treasury as well as a portion of the agricultural products of each covenanted land of your domain, for the most distant of them (i.e. living far away from the capital) has an equal right to that of the nearest of them (i.e. living in the capital) and you have been charged with guarding the rights of each one of them.[47] Let not any arrogance make you heedless of them, for you will not be excused for neglecting even a trifling matter on account of your having had dealt sufficiently with the more important ones. Do not cast away your anxiety for them nor turn a haughty face towards them; look after the problems of him who cannot reach you from among them and those who the eyes [of the people] deride and are treated with contempt. Particularly appoint for them (i.e. destitute people) one from among your trusted officers as are God-fearing, humble and modest and let him bring their wants to your notice.

Treat them (the destitute) in such a way that God may forgive you on the day you meet Him, for of all the subjects these (destitute) stand more in need of justice (i.e. benevolent treatment) than the others, although you should do your best in paying each his due.

Take particular care of the orphans and the feeble old men who have no resources (i.e. means of livelihood) for themselves but do not like to go about begging. This is no doubt a hard task for the governors,[48] but every right thing is hard to do; and God makes it easy for those people[49] who seek the life Hereafter, accustom themselves to patience and trust in the truth of the promise of God made to them.

Public Audience and Open Conferences:

Assign a part of your time for the needy in which you may be free to deal with them (i.e. with their problems) personally and sit for them in public audience, showing due humility to God who has created you. [On such occasions] keep away from them your soldiers, your aides from among the members of your guard and your police officers, so that each one of them[50] may speak without reserve and fearlessly, for I have heard the Prophet of God, peace be upon him, say on more than one occasion: "No nation shall ever be blessed in which the right of the weak is not wrested from the strong without fear (or favor)."

Bear patiently with the foolish, the uncouth[51] and the inarticulate[52] from among them. Do not allow yourself to be annoyed or angry with them or to be rude and arrogant to them (because of their ill-manners and harshness), for God will thereby bestow on you generously His mercy and make incumbent on you the reward of His obedience. What ever you can give them, give it cheerfully and ungrudgingly; and if you (have to) refuse, (their excessive demands) do it in a pleasant and apologetic manner.

Then there are certain things (i.e. duties) which you have to perform personally. One of these is writing replies to your officials when your secretaries are unable to do so,[53] another is to issue prompt orders for [fulfilling] the requirements (or meeting the grievances) of the people on the same day as they come to your notice and your assistants are reluctant to do so. Perform each day's work that very day, for every day has its own assignment.

Communion with God:

Set apart the best of your time for communion with God and prolong these periods for yourself, although every moment of yours (spent in performing your state duties) is for God, provided it is spent with good intention and (during which) your subjects are safe and secure (i.e. happy with your rule and safe from oppression).

The special act by which you may purify your religion for God is the performance of those duties[54] which are exclusively for Him. So submit yourself to God during the day and the night and perform fully the acts of devotion by which you seek the proximity of God without any let or hindrance, however heavy· be your physical exertion.

When you get up to offer prayers with the people (i.e. lead the prayers) do not scare them [by making it so lengthy] nor waste or dissipate it [by making it too short] for there may be among them some who are ill or have some work to do. I asked the Prophet of God, peace be upon him, when he sent me out to Yemen "How should I pray with the people?" And he replied "Pray with them like the praying of the weakest of them and be compassionate to the believers."

The Rulers should not live in isolation from the Subjects:

After all I have said so far, bear one more thing in mind. Do not remain aloof from your subjects, for the isolation of governors from their subjects causes a kind of narrowness and lack of knowledge about their conditions. This isolation of governors from their subjects moreover prevents the latter from learning of that about which they have not been (properly) informed, with the result that a small thing appears to be big to them and a big thing small, what is good (right) seems to be bad (wrong) and what is bad seems to be good and (consequently) the truth is mixed up with falsehood. The governor (too) after all is a human being and does not know what things the people conceal from him. There are no distinguishing marks on what is right by which one may discern the various forms of truth from falsehood. You are only one of these two (kinds of) men (i.e. rulers): either you are a man who is generous and diligent in giving the people what is their due and so why should you conceal yourself while rendering the people their due or while performing a noble act? Or, you are a man afflicted with stinginess; and in that case how quickly would the people abstain from making any request to you when they have become despondent of your generosity. And then most of the requirements of the people entail no burden on you, since they are of the nature of either a complaint against some injustice or a demand for justice in certain matters.

There are usually a number of intimate and privileged companions around the governors, who are often selfish and aggressive and do not observe justice in their dealings. You should uproot these people by putting an end to the causes of that situation (i.e. corruption). Do not allot any estate to any one of your courtiers or close friends and relations. They must never expect from you the grant of a fief which might do harm to those who live in its neighborhood in such matters as irrigation or any other common work, the burden of which they may pass on to other men and the profit therefrom would go to them and not to the state while the blame for it would come to you in this world as well as in the Hereafter.

Impose whatever rights and obligations are due on those who would bear them whether they be near or distant (i.e. close to you as friends and relations or strangers having no connection with you). Do this patiently and judiciously, irrespective of what your near relations and bosom friends may think about it; and look forward to its result, even though it may weigh heavily upon you, for the consequence of it will be praiseworthy for you. If the subjects suspect any injustice in you, come out before them with your excuse (i.e. put your case before them) and remove their suspicions by making things clear to them. In this way you will discipline yourself[55] and also make you gentle and kind to your subjects. And thus by doing your best for your subjects you will also attain your desire of keeping them firmly on the right path.

Peace and Treaties:

Never miss the chance for a peaceful settlement to which your enemy invites you while God is also pleased with it, for in peace lies the comfort of your soldiers, a relief for you from your anxieties and tranquility and prosperity for your territory. But take all possible precautions against the enemy after the conclusion of peace with him, for the enemy often becomes friendly in order to make a surprise attack. Exercise prudence, therefore and remain wary after your good faith [is placed in them] in this matter.

If you make a pact with your enemy or make any promise to him, honor your promise by fulfilling it and observe your pact honestly. Make your own life a shield[56] for what you have granted [according to the terms of the treaty] to your enemy; for on none of the prescriptions of God are all men, in spite of their different inclinations and diverse opinions more united than on honoring a promise. This was in fact the practice even of the polytheists in their dealings with one another, though not with the Muslims, since they had found the consequences of treachery to be very unwholesome. So then never betray your trust or break your promise and also do not deceive your enemy, for no one can dare go against God except for the ignorant and the wretched. Indeed, God has made His promise and His trust a [messenger of] peace which He has mercifully extended to all men and a sanctuary in the protection of which they find comfort and asylum; a shelter which they seek eagerly. There should therefore be no deception, no fraud and no treachery in treaties and pacts of peace.[57]

Do not make any pact in which there is room for subterfuge and do not try to take advantage of any equivoke [in your favor] once the treaty has been confirmed and ratified.[58] Do not be tempted to seek unrightfully the revocation of a pact which God has made binding upon you due to any inconvenient [clause] in it. For indeed, your patience with a difficult situation [caused by the treaty] which you hope will ultimately be dispelled and end up in your favor [if you break it] is better than a betrayal, the consequence of which you dread. Moreover, [because of breaking a pact] you will have to answer to God and your life here as well as in the hereafter will become wretched.[59]

Bloodshed and Murder are the Worst Crimes:

Beware of shedding blood unlawfully; for nothing brings more hate, is more serious in its consequences, is quicker to cause the disappearance of one's bliss or terminate the duration of rule than the shedding of blood unlawfully.

The first thing which God, the Glorious, will take up with His slaves on the Day of Resurrection would be to give His judgment about the blood shed by them. And therefore do not try to strengthen your power (i.e. rule) by spilling blood unlawfully, for shedding innocent blood not only weakens your power but may also destroy it or transfer it to someone else.

You shall not be excused by God or by me for having willfully committed murder, for that entails a bodily indemnity (death penalty). And if you have been guilty of some mistake (i.e. if you have injured or killed somebody by mistake), or your whip, your sword or your hand might have exceeded the limit of your intention (i.e. while carrying out legal penalties), for even a blow with the hand may cause death, then let not the arrogance of your authority make you too vain to pay the near relations of the murdered man their due indemnity (the bloodwit).[60]

The last Word: What is Required of a Ruler:

Beware and do not be conceited nor be overconfident in yourself (i.e. of whatever good qualities you may find in you or good deeds you have performed) nor be fond of extravagant praise (flattery), because these things provide the most trustworthy opportunities to the Devil to ruin whatever kindness or good deeds there might have occurred from the benevolent persons.

Beware of holding your subjects under obligation to you for your kindness, exaggerating what you have done, or making a promise to them and then breaking it; for to consider others under obligation to oneself obliterates the kind act,[61] exaggeration takes away the light of truth and breach of promise earns hate from both God and men. God, the Exalted has said *"It is very hateful to God that you say what you do not do."*[62]

Avoid haste in all affairs before their proper time or laxity about them when they can be (promptly) dealt with, persisting in them when they are found to be undesirable or showing weakness about them when they are clear and manifest (i.e. once a course of action becomes clear do not waste time). In short, put everything in its proper place and do every act at the right time for it.

Refrain from appropriating to yourself what should be shared equally by all men. Do not be negligent of what you should be concerned with and is clear to the eyes (i.e. the glaring mistakes made by your administration). Because what you have taken shall be taken away from you by someone else and soon the curtain shall be lifted from all affairs and you shall be called upon to provide to him who has been treated unjustly by you.

Control your sense of pride, your fits of anger, the violence of your hand and the sharpness of your tongue. Guard against these (vices) by restraining hasty words (i.e. abusive remarks) and delaying punitive action until your anger has cooled and you gain complete control over yourself. You shall never be in a position to accustom your mind to [all] this except by increasing your anxiety by remembering your return to your Lord (i.e. unless you constantly remember that you have to return to God and that this fear overcomes all other thoughts).

It is incumbent upon you to think of a just rule or an excellent practice of those who lived in the past before your time, as also the example of our Prophet, peace be upon him and the members of his family, or the duties prescribed in the Book of God and then to follow that you have observed us doing in this respect. Thus exert yourself to the best of your ability to act in accordance with what I have advised you in this epistle of mine so that there may be no weakness on your part at the time when your heart is tempted by its carnal desires.

I beseech God by His limitless Compassion and by His supreme Might to grant [us] every desirable thing, to guide me as well as you to what He is pleased with, namely persisting in justice towards Him and His creatures,[63] together with a good reputation among the people and beautiful memorials in the country, the perfection of bliss and the augmentation of honor. I beg Him also to bring my life as well as yours to a close with good fortune and with martyrdom. Verily, we have to return to him.

Peace be on the Prophet of God."

Notes and References
Chapter Four

1. Before every oration or letter the compiler always uses the preposition *min* (from), indicating that what has reached him might not be complete, or that he is reproducing a select passage from a much larger text.

2. See Introduction.

3. *'Ahid* means contract, obligation, responsibility, vow, oath, will, covenant and bequest. It is also used for the diploma of investiture or letter of appointment given by rulers and caliphs to their governors at the time of the latter's appointments and it is in the last two meanings in which the word *'ahid* is used here. We would, however, prefer to use the shortest single word 'bequest' which is also quite comprehensive in this context.

4. Aggressors against the territorial integrity and safety of Egypt, as well as those who try to disturb internal peace and take over control of the province from the legal authority in power.

5. *Fara'id* means what has been explicitly made obligatory such as the *salat, sawm, hajj* etc; but the word *sunan* when referring to God is rather difficult to translate. The phrase *sunnat al-Allah* occurs in the Qur'an several times, such as 33:62, 35:43 and passim, and has variously been translated as, 'ways', 'conduct' and also 'rules' referring to the *Shari'a*.

6. *Wa an yansurul Allah subhanahu biqalbihi wa yadihi wa lisanihi*–'to help God with the heart' indicates belief in the Truth, 'with hand', means *Jihad* in the way of Allah and 'with the tongue' means "establishing good and prohibiting evil."

7. cf. The Qur'an, 22:40—"*God will certainly help those, who help His (cause).*"

8. The best way to do justice to one's self and to keep it out of harm is to restrain from committing vice and from things which the self inordinately and irrationally desires.

9. As far as the administration of justice is concerned both the believers and the non-believers or Muslims and non-Muslims are equal as human beings; no distinction should be made on the basis of religion only.

10. By way of resorting to injustice and tyranny to your subjects who are the creatures of God.

11. Do not act hastily when you are over-whelmed by anger or passion, and can avoid it by exercising a little patience.

12. *Gharb* literally means edge of a sword and its sharpness or the extreme point of something and is also used for going beyond the limits or bonds. Here it signifies extreme anger or one extremely conceited with strength and power. See Ibn Abi'l-Hadid, *Sharh*, v. xvii: 34; also Lane, *An Arabic-English Lexicon*.

13. *Insif Allah* to do justice to God means not to disobey His commands in all affairs of life and conduct and not to violate the responsibilities laid down upon you by God in respect to yourself as well as your subjects.

14. Do not be partial in the administration of justice to your friends and favorites from among the subjects.

15. Neither too harsh nor too lenient.

16. The governor is not supposed to probe into the personal weaknesses or shortcomings of the people which they themselves hide from others. There must be a difference in the eyes of the governor between the personal defects and the defects which have a bearing on the social life of the community.

17. cf. The Quran, 58:22—"*Nor it is for Me to take as helpers such as lead (men) astray*"; and The Qur'an, 18:51—"*You will not find any people who believe in God and the last Day, loving those who resist God and His Apostle.*"

18. *Bitana* literally means inner side or lining of a garment and is also used for entourage or a sub-tribe; here it signifies intimate companionship.

19. Most preferable to enjoy your fullest confidence and trust in matters of state and its affairs.

20. *Awliya* sing. *wali* literally, to be near or the near ones, hence a friend. *Wali* is usually translated as 'the friend of God' (a saint or a pious person).

21. That a ruler can create goodwill among his subjects and can make them faithful and sincere to him only when he is kind and considerate to them.

22. *Nasab-an tawila*, lit. prolonged anxiety. Here it means that when a ruler fails to cultivate goodwill and confidence among his subjects, he can never enjoy peace of mind and will keep on worrying about the affairs of the state.

23. *Ma'aqid*, lit. contracting parties, indicate that the judges and government officers concerned settle the disputes regarding

business, taxes and other financial matters. They also guard the rights and privileges of the citizens.

24. *Bi aydihim* refers to the blacksmiths, carpenters, masons etc., who work with their hands to cater to the needs of others.

25. In Abduh's edition it reads *wa alqahum jayb-an*, but in Ibn Abi'l Hadid's and Muhammad Abu'l Fadl's editions it is *wa atharahum jayb-an* which seems to be more correct and is explained as "the one who is the most trustworthy, honest and free of any corruption or dishonesty." *Taharat al jayb* (lit. cleanliness of the pocket) is a beautiful expression for the honesty of a person as against the pocket of a thief who puts stolen goods in it. Here, according to 'Abduh, it indicates both cleanliness of heart as well as of material things. I have however taken its implied meaning as 'character'.

26. The term *muruwwa* represents a moral, ethical and cultural institution coming down from pre-Islamic Arabia which was adapted with a somewhat different connotation and emphasis in the Islamic period. It is commonly and rather conveniently translated as "virtue" but in fact it is almost impossible to render it in a word or phrase into another language. *Muruwwa* signifies all those virtues which founded in the tradition of a people, constitute the fame of an individual or the tribe to which he belongs; the observance of those duties which are connected with family ties, the relationships of protection and hospitality and the virtues of honour, courage, fortitude and strength. In Islam it denotes more the Islamic virtues than the pagan ones. For a detailed discussion of its meaning see. Lane, *An Arabic-English Lexicon*, p. 2702. Mubarrad, *al-Kamil*, ed. Muhammad Abu'l Fadl, Egypt, n.d., vol. i, p. 47; Ibn 'Abd Rabbih, *al-'Iqdal-farid*, ed. Ahmad Amin, et al, Cairo 1967, vol. ii, pp. 292 f., and by far the best analysis in Ignaz Goldziher, *Muslim Studies*, (tr.) London 1967, vol. i, pp. 22 ff.

27. For its meaning and conception see Ibn Qutayba, *Rasa'il alBu-laghia*, ed. Kurd 'Ali, Cairo, n.d., p. 360; Abu'l Faraj al-Isfahani, *Kitab al-Aghani*, Beirut 1973, vol. i, p. 45; and a fuller discussion of it in Jafri, S.H.M., *Origins and Early Development of Shi'a Islam*, London 1979, pp. 4ff, and Goldziher, op. cit., pp. 40 ff.

28. For its meaning and importance in Arabian society see, e.g. Ibn Durayd, *Kitab al-Ishtiqaq*, ed. Wustenfeld, Gottingen 1854, pp. 238 f; *Aghani*, v.xix, p. 128; *'Iqd*, v. iii, pp. 313, 333 ff; Jafri, op. cit., pp. 6ff.

29. The responsibilities of the parents is not only to provide material needs of their children but also to look after their character building and moral behavior. Thus 'Ali's advice to the governor to look after the soldiers as the parents look after their children, includes both material as well as moral welfare.

30. Do not neglect small favors to them thinking that these are too trivial for your status to handle them and that you have done enough in tackling serious problems; then why should you bother about small things.

31. Has an importance for them, though for you it may be too small.

32. The Qur'an, 4:59.

33. People of excellent character, superior caliber and meritorious record.

34. The judge should not be satisfied with ordinary enquiry or scrutiny of case but must go deep into all its aspects. In other words a judge must not be an easy-going person but must exert himself to find out the truth.

35. Should not accept any pressure and must be impartial and do his duty without fear, favors or prejudice.

36. The position of a judge should be so high that none can even dream of coveting it and dare not speak ill of him before you.

37. You should hold your judges in such a high esteem that none of your courtiers or officers, however great they might be, could lord over them or do them any harm. Thus the judiciary must be above every kind of pressure or influence from the executive and must be free from fear or favor, intrigue or backbiting. This is possible only when they are accorded the highest position by the governor.

38. The term *dīn* which is used here is so comprehensive in its meaning and applicability that it is almost impossible to render it exactly with any single word or phrase; it can only be explained. Islam as a whole is called *Dīn* which comprises both beliefs and practices and thus *Dīn* embraces all aspects of religion whether in relation to God or that of human institutions. In the Qur'an both *shari'a* and *dīn* are used in correlative sense and thus *Dīn* is the total sum of the *Shari'a*. However, in the Arabic language *Dīn* also means power, authority, management. All these meanings in essence refer to 'the code of law' given by God to govern all human affairs whether temporal or religious. Nothing could be a better word to be used in this context than *dīn*.

39. They used the power and authority vested in them for amassing wealth and the satisfaction of their pleasures.

40. After paying them handsomely enough for a comfortable living if they prove dishonest or disloyal then you have the right to punish them.

41. If they know that they are being watched secretly they will refrain from dishonesty, misrule, malpractice and tyranny over their subjects.

42. '*Amarat al-ard* means both cultivation, fertility and the enriching of land, as well as inhabiting and populating it.

43. Such rulers or officials want to accumulate as much wealth as they can by any possible means because they are always afraid that their rule might not last long. They never learn any lesson from the past history of nations and the causes of their downfall.

44. '*Umur* here refers to the confidential matters of the ruler.

45. They should be men of exemplary character, intelligent and capable enough to look after the interest of the State.

46. In 'Abduh's edition it reads *wa husn-i hadithahim*, which I have translated here as "their pleasant conversation." In Abu'l Fadl's and some other editions it reads *wa husn-i khidmatahim*, which would mean "their serving you pleasantly and efficiently." To me Abduh's text makes better sense.

47. You should not be negligent of those of the poor and the needy who live far away from the capital in distant places of the province. They have the same rights as those living nearby. The rights of the two should be equal in your eyes.

48. To keep trace of them. Either because of their being children or weak and feeble due to old age, or because of the fact that they are averse to seeking alms they cannot reach the governor. It is therefore the duty of the governor to reach them.

49. The word *aqwam* here is explained in the following paragraph.

50. *Mutakallihum* may also mean their spokesmen or representatives.

51. *Al-kharq* is used here for ignorant, unskillful, clumsy, ill-mannered or foolish.

52. *Al-'ayy* signifies those who cannot express themselves properly.

53. That is, such replies to the letters of officers which are either beyond the jurisdiction of your secretaries or who are unable to attend to these delicate matters.

54. *Fara'id* (obligations), in this context refers specially to the prayers, five times a day.

55. Your mind will become attuned to the sense of justice.

56. If necessary, you must even stake your own life on the fulfilment of the promises given to and the terms settled with the enemy.

57. Any deception or fraud against an enemy after having made a treaty with him is tantamount to deception against God, which only a wretched or an ignorant person would dare to do.

58. Do not use such words or phrases in the pact which may be interpreted in more than one way. It must be free of ambiguities and should be in clear language, giving no chance for misinterpretation or reinterpretation.

59. If any clause of the treaty, after having been concluded, makes you face certain difficulties, do not try to break the treaty; you can never be sure of the results. Moreover, a violation of the treaty obligation may bring upon you the wrath of God. Thus it is far better for you to wait in patience for a wholesome result to follow than to break it out of any apprehension. Finally, 'Ali emphasizes the sanctity of promises.

60. If on any account the corporal punishment meted out by the governor for any lesser crime results in the death of the guilty, let not the position and prestige of the governor let them refuse to pay the due compensation (*qisas* or *diyat*) to the heirs of the deceased.

78

61. cf. The Qur'an, 2:264—"*O you who believe, do not obliterate your charity by reminders of your generosity.*"

62. The Qur'an, 61:3.

63. To enable us to successfully plead our case before God and justify our deeds before the people.

"And turn not your face from people in contempt;
Nor walk in insolence through the earth,
For God loves not any arrogant boaster."

(The Quran, 31:18)

CHAPTER FIVE

'Ali's Letter to his Governor in Basra

Introductory note by al-Sharif al-Radi

> From a letter of 'Ali, peace be upon him, addressed to 'Uthman bin Hunayf al-Ansari, his governor in Basra when he heard that 'Uthman was invited to the wedding of some people from among its citizens and that he went to the feast.

"After the due praise of God, O' Ibn Hunayf I have come to know how you were invited by a man from the young men of the citizens of Basra to a feast and how you hastened to go it, choice dishes being prepared for you and platters of food being served to you.

I never thought that you would accept [an invitation to] a feast given by a people, from which the poor had been barred from it and only the rich invited. So look what you are eating from that food and if there be anything the knowledge of which may be doubtful to you (i.e. whether it is earned by unlawful means), throw it away and eat only of that which appears to have been lawfully acquired.

Listen, for every subject there is a ruler whom he follows and from the effulgence of whose knowledge he obtains light. And behold, your ruler (Ali) has protected himself from the elements with his two rags[1] and takes for his food only two loaves of bread. Indeed, you cannot do this; but you can at least help me with piety, effort, chastity and rectitude;[2] for by God, I have not hoarded from the world any gold, have not collected any wealth from its treasures, have not prepared any clothes to replace my rags, have not possessed of its land a single span[3] and have not taken from its food except that much as would suffice someone with a wounded back;[4] one who eats very little. And indeed the world in my sight is more worthless and insignificant than the bitter fruit of the oak tree.

Yes, we had in our possession [the estate of] Fadak[5] from among all that the sky overshadows, but the minds of some people grudged it to us, while the minds of certain others were generous about it; and the best arbitrator is God! And what shall I do with Fadak or with anything other than Fadak (i.e. wealth or property of this world), while my dwelling tomorrow is going to be the grave, when my very existence and all its traces will come to an end in its darkness; and all news about it would disappear; and a pit, (i.e. grave) which even though the hands of its digger increase its width, would be choked up by stones and bricks and its opening would be blocked up by layers upon layers of dust. And therefore, it is for me to train my own self in piety, so that it may emerge safe on the day of the great fear (i.e. the Day of Judgment) and remain firm and steady on the edge of the slippery bridge.[6]

Had I so wished (being the ruler of a fabulous empire) I could have found my way to purified honey and the best portion of wheat as well as fabrics of silk (i.e. worldly pleasures and luxuries). But God forbid that my desire may overpower me and my greed lead me to choose choice foods when perhaps in the Hijaz or al-Yamama there is one who does not hope to get even a loaf of bread and has never experienced satiation! Shall I pass the night with my stomach full of food while there are around me hungry stomachs and burning livers; or that I may be as the poet has said:

> "It is shameful enough that you spend the night with a full stomach, while around you are livers which long for a leather strap."[7]

Shall I be content that it may be said of me: "He is the commander of the Believers," and not share with them the unpleasant things of the world, or be for them a model of austere living? For I have not been created to be engrossed in eating wholesome foods like a tethered beast whose only concern is its fodder or like another animal let loose, the only occupation of which is grazing, filling up its belly with the grasses it feeds upon being heedless of what is required of it; or that I may be left unguarded and left neglected without any purpose; or that I may trail the rope of misguidance and plunge into the path of bewilderment.

I can almost hear one of you saying: "If this be the food of the Son of Abu Talib ('Ali), it would render him too weak to fight his adversaries[8] and challenge the brave warriors." Listen, a wild tree is harder of wood while the green plants are softer of skin; and the trees fed by only the rain burn more strongly and die out more slowly. And I and the Prophet of God are like two plants having the same root or like the arm and the shoulder.

By God, if the Arabs all unite together to fight me, I shall not turn away from them and if I am given an opportunity to do so, I shall hasten to cut off their heads. I shall certainly soon try to purge the land of these perverse persons and this inverted body,[9] as the gravel may be removed from the grains of the harvested crop.

Keep off from me, O world; for your reins are on your shoulder. I have escaped out of your talons, have slipped away from your snares and have avoided your pitfalls.

Where are the generations whom your (world) deluded with your playful ways? Where are nations whom you charmed with your baubles? Here they lie in their graves and pledged to their Sepulchral niches. By God (O world), if you were a visible person and a body capable of feeling[10] I would have subjected you to the punishment prescribed by God for the sake of those men whom you have deluded with false hopes, those nations which you have thrown into the abyss and those kings whom you have handed over to destruction and brought to the sources of trial from which no one returns after having come to drink at them.

Alas! He who treads upon your slippery ground slips and he who embarks on your deep waters is drowned; but he who turns aside from your snares is guided by God. The man who escaped you does not mind if his resting place be narrow (i.e. he is poor and is denied of worldly things) since the world in his sight is like a day, the end of which is approaching fast.

Go away from me (O World), for by God, I shall not submit to you that you may humiliate me and shall not be obedient to you that you may lead me!

And I swear by God, making an exception in my oath for the will of God, that I shall surely give myself such a training that I will show happiness at a loaf of bread, though dry, which it can get; and will be content with a food seasoned only with salt and shall leave my eye with its tears exhausted, like a spring of water the flow of which has dried up. Shall I become like the grazing camels who fill up with their fodder and sit down, or like the goats who eat their green herbage and lie down to rest—and so shall 'Ali eat of his provisions and go to sleep?

May then his eye become dead when after sixty long years [of his life] he imitates the cattle let loose and the grazing animals guarded by their herd.

Happy is the one who renders to God His due, bears patiently his miseries, discards his sleep in the night so that when drowsiness over-comes him, he lies down on the ground and makes a pillow of his hand! He is one of those men whose eyes are made sleepless by the fear of their next life, whose sides eschew their beds, whose lips pronounce in low tones the name of their Lord and whose sins are wiped off by their prolonged begging for forgiveness: "Behold, the partisans of God are the ones who attain salvation."[11]

So fear God, O son of Hunayf and be contented with your won loaves of bread so that you may win your release from hell-fire."

Notes and References
Chapter Five

1. *Timr*, pl. *Atmar*, means an old, worn out or tattered garment or rag which is divided in two; one to cover the lower body and

the other for covering the shoulders.

2.   'Ali means to say that even though it is not possible for you to practise that frugality and self-denial which I am able to do, you can try to follow me by exerting yourself to attain righteousness and piety.

3.   *Shibr-un min al-ard*, an Arabic idiom meaning "a foot of land."

4.   *Dabira*, literally meaning a beast of burden, especially a she-ass; who after being wounded can eat only very little.

5.   Fadak, an oasis and rich agricultural land in the northern Hijaz near Khaybar, two or three days journey from Medina, became the personal property of the Prophet as his share of the booty. The Prophet used to spend the revenues of Fadak on his family, the needy and the poor of the Banu Hashim and on the wayfarers. After the death of the Prophet, the estate of Fadak became an object of serious dispute between the only surviving daughter of the Prophet, Fatima who claimed it as her inheritance; and the first Caliph, Abu Bakr. Fatima's claim to the estate was rejected by the Caliph on the grounds that the property of the Prophet belongs to the state and not to the family. 'Ali and Fatima thus lost the estate of Fadak. For a detailed account of the dispute see Ibn Sa'd: *Tabaqat*, vol. 11, pp. 314 ff; Ya'qubi, *Tarikh*, vol. 11, p.127; Ibn 'Abd al-Barr, *Isti'ab*, vol. II, p. 571. Also cf. Vaglieri, *Encyclopedia of Islam* (2nd ed), article "Fadak."

6.   An allusion to the symbolic bridge which every one has to cross on the Day of Judgment. cf. Winsinck: *Handbook of Muhammadan Traditions*, s.v. Bridge.

7.   Hatam al-Ta'i, cf. Ibn Abil-Hadid, *Sharh*, vol. XVI, p. 288.

8.   Reference to Mu'awiya, who rebelled against him and organized his Syrian armies to fight him.

9. *Shakhs al-Maʿkus*, literally a perverse person, means one who has changed his beliefs and has stubbornly adopted wrong in place of right; and *Jism al-Markus*: literally, inverted body, signifying a person who has gone completely astray and has changed truth into falsehood. It is a reference to the Qur'anic verse *"God has upset them for their evil deeds"* (4:88). See Ibn Abil Hadid, v. XVI, pp. 291 f.

10. *Qalib-an Hissiyan* is used here for the world which cannot be identified as a person or a body with senses and feelings and which can be made an object of punishment.

11. The Qur'an, 58:22.

Section Three

Morality and Conduct of Life in Islam

*"It is not righteousness that you turn your face to the East
and the West, but righteous is he who believes in Allah
and the Last Day and the Angels and the Scripture
and the Prophets and gives his wealth for the love of Him,
to kinsfolk and to orphans and the needy and the wayfarer And to those who
ask, and to set slaves free; And observes
proper worship and pays the poor-due;
And those who keep their treaty when they make one,
And patient in tribulation and adversity and time of stress.
Such are they who are sincere; such are the God-fearing."*

(The Qur'an 2:177)

CHAPTER SIX

Ali's Testament to his Son

I. *Introduction*

The science of morality and ethics is commonly defined as that which concerns the distinction between right and wrong, good and evil or a system of values on which a society is built and functions; hence conduct or behavior. Taken in this sense, there have always been two schools of thought about the concept and nature of morality as it worked in human society throughout history.

One school asserts that morality originally developed independently of religion and is by its very nature autonomous and self-sustained. This school of thought brings to its support apparently convincing arguments from history and a mass of equally convincing data from the recently developed science of anthropology. The gods of savages are not moral and are not concerned with human society; they are worshipped and propitiated because they are believed to control the processes of nature. It is only in a more developed society that it is realized that if the moral impulse is valid, it must derive from some moral element in the universe. Then begins the slow process of the moralization of religious ideas. The saying "a good man is the noblest work of God and a good God is the noblest work of man"[1], is not merely an irreverent jest: rightly understood, it epitomizes the evolution of religious thought from fetishism to moral monotheism. The religion of classical antiquity, with its all-too-human gods was less than half way along the road to this point and the root cause of its decline under the criticism of philosophers and its ultimate collapse under the impact of higher religions was the growing realization of its incompatibility with the highest moral ideals. It was a moral issue again on which the Hebrew prophets challenged their priesthood; and so was the case with the emergence of Christianity and of Islam. In short, according to this school, moral intuition is not the result of belief in any particular religion; it is direct and fundamental and no philosophical or theological system which is not compatible with it will, in the long run be accepted as true by intelligent men.

This view is not, however, without some truth to it; and even in Islam, one of the two most important schools of thought (the Mu'tazilites) to a great extent, subscribe to the idea of the autonomous and fundamental character of morality standing independently of religious belief. The Mu'tazilites' stand, it must be pointed out was not that of the secularists but was on a different plane and for different reasons, mainly influenced by Aristotelian rationalism. We are however concerned here neither with the purely scientific or secularist approach to morality nor with the theoretical discussions of philosophers about the nature of the *summum bonum*.

The other school of thought connects morality inseparably to religion. To them, religious belief has always been the mainstay of morality. Religion, whether in its most primitive or most advanced form is as old as man himself and so is the concept of morality; thus both religion and morality by their very nature are essentially synonymous terms. Perhaps that was what Matthew Arnold had in mind when he said "Religion is morality touched with emotion."[2]

It is no doubt a fact that ethics as a science was first developed by the Greeks; but as languages existed long before someone developed the terminology to understand and clarify the principles on which the language had been unconsciously constructed, so man's perception of the difference between good and evil preceded the science of ethics by millennia. As language is a natural product of human society, so is his morality; the difference between good and evil springs from human relations. Religion and morality have therefore been advancing or receding either in parallel or in interaction with each other. Scientifically, ethics is discussed separately from religious belief or metaphysical presumptions, but any thorough discussion of the ultimate nature of the 'ideal', which determines our sense of good or evil, forces us to define our belief in the ultimate reality in which our lives are rooted and from which they spring. Thus in Islam, like Judaism and Christianity and in most major religions with certain differences in detail, morality does not stand by itself, but flows directly religious belief.

In all major religions, the authentic code of morality is derived from the basic source of that religion. In religions which have no claim to the revealed scriptures such as Zoroastrianism and Buddhism, the moral code is derived from the teachings of their founders–Zoroaster and Buddha–preserved and handed down by their closest disciples. In religions which have revealed scriptures, their moral code is taken from the sacred books, such is the case with Judaism, Christianity and Islam. In Islam, thus, the main source of the moral code is the Qur'an, the Word of God, revealed to His last Prophet Muhammad. As God chose Muhammad as the recipient of His revelation and as the messenger of His command (*rasūl*), the Prophet naturally becomes the first and the most perfect model of that moral conduct which God has laid down for the mankind; thus, *"you have, indeed, in the person of the Prophet the best and the most beautiful model of conduct (to follow)."*[3] This makes the Prophet's own behavior and conduct the second fundamental source of moral conduct in Islam; this is known as the *Sunna* or the life-pattern of the Prophet. In other words, the essence of morality in Islam, as repeatedly emphasized by the Qur'an, is epitomized in two fundamental aspects; faith (*imān*) and virtuous deeds or action (*'amal salih*), the first being supplied by the Qur'an, the other exemplified by the Prophet. The entire structure of the moral code in Islam thus springs from these two sources.

Then comes the second phase, when the basic code or fundamental principles of morality supplied by the revealed books and the teachings of the prophets are faithfully conveyed, with their own interpretations by the companions and the close disciples of the Messengers to their people and to the generations that follow. Judaism was interpreted and conveyed to the people by those trained and left behind by Moses, Christianity was taught by the disciples of Jesus Christ. This has also been the case with other major religions other than the Abrahamic religions, such as Zoroastrianism and Buddhism. These interpretations of the close disciples or the first and most devoted followers over the course of time acquire great importance in the internal development of these religions and receive the status of authentic exegesis of the sacrosanct texts and the precepts of the prophets or founders of these religions.[4] In Islam too, the closest companions and disciples of the Prophet devotedly and zealously took upon themselves the task of teaching the people the message of the Qur'an and the *sunnah* of the Prophet.

It is in this context that we present here in English translation a document on morality and the conduct of life, which 'Ali b. Abi Talib wrote in the form of a testament for his son al-Hasan,[5] in the year 657 A.D. (37 A.H.). 'Ali's closest relationship to the Prophet and his most devotion to Islam cannot be overemphasized. Suffice it to say that he was not only the cousin and son-in-law of the Prophet, but was brought up from childhood by the Prophet himself. Before the call, he witnessed every moment of Muhammad's life as one of the closest members of his family and after the call he was the first among them to embrace Islam, along with Khadija, the Prophet's first wife. 'Ali and Islam thus grew together. In short, his character, his way of thinking, his outlook on life, his habits and indeed his entire personality became an embodiment of the teachings of the Qur'an and the *sunnah* of the Prophet. The testament given below, can therefore be taken as the best and most faithful elaboration of the Islamic ideal of life and morality.

It is difficult to discuss in any detail in this introduction even the most important points of this precious epistle on morality and the conduct of life. If we, however, try to define morality in the light of this testament, we may say that to 'Ali, morality means how a man should lead a *meaningful* life in relation to himself, his fellow men or his society, the natural phenomena he is surrounded with and above all, in relation to his Creator, the Omnipotent and the Omniscient—God. In other words, the entire testament rotates round four fundamental aspects of human relationships: (1) man's relationship with God, (2) with himself, (3) with his fellow man; and (4) with Nature.

We are greatly tempted to discuss all four aspects one by one, quoting relevant passages from the testament, but we must restrain ourselves as it will make this introduction too lengthy to be accommodated in these pages. However, an overall impression one gets from the testament is that in the mind of 'Ali, a meaningful or moral life in Islam is one which finds complete harmony in all of these four relationships. The harmony 'Ali wants to attain is not merely a harmony in action, as in primitive religions; nor it is only a moral or spiritual harmony, as in the great religions of the Middle and Near East; nor is the harmony sought more than a harmony; a complete and final identity, as in most of the religions of India and the Far East. But it it this harmony 'Ali seeks is a comprehensive, integrated harmony in all aspects and all relationships.

Islam is thus a religion of complete integration. For the first time in history, we see the doctrine of the development of the whole man in complete integration with himself, with society and with nature, this integration being based on the belief in a single Creator who is the unity of all existence. Moral action then must be motivated by fostering and cherishing and by creating ever richer harmonies of existence. Good is that which has a tendency to multiply; and evil is destructive of others as well as of itself. 'Ali tells us that the purpose of life is to live in a manner that is progressively purified, edified, enriched, strengthened, elevated and harmonized. At the same time, throughout the testament 'Ali reminds us of the fact that life is full of conflicts within and without. In every phase of it there is a battlefield. The struggle of good against evil is an essential and inevitable fact of human existence. Life in a phenomenal setting offers harmonies as well as disharmonies and the purpose of human existence and the object of all moral struggle is to overcome disharmonies, either correcting or ending them. Once a man achieves harmony in all his relations he attains peace; that peace is Islam.

Islam means peace as well as submission to the will of God. Submission to God implies in attitude and in action a regulation of our lives. God, according to Islam, is not a dogma but an ideal, a regulative force of life and a guarantee of our highest values. Thus, submission to God, the 'Ideal', with a firm belief in its reality is a life of both virtue and inner happiness. A man who submits himself to God is true to his real self and therefore attains inner peace which is real happiness and is quite different from worldly pleasures. This real happiness more than compensates for any lack of material gain or physical pain and suffering.

The virtues of Aristotle's 'Ethics' and 'Politics' (justice, temperance, fortitude and prudence) were all qualities valuable for building and improving society and civic life. They relate to purely worldly conditions and demands. In Islam as interpreted by 'Ali in the light of the Qur'an, a quite different set of qualities comes to the fore. It begins with the key-note:

> I advise you, O my son! to fear God, and to stick to His commands, to fill up your heart with His remembrance and to clutch firmly at His rope; for which link or connection if you clasp it is more trustworthy than the link between you and your Lord? Revive your heart (i.e. self) with admonition and kill it (i.e. its inordinate desires) by piety and abstinence, strengthen it with the firm and unwavering belief (*yaqin*) and brighten it up with wisdom (*hikma*) subjugate it by the (constant) remembrance of death and make it acknowledge the mortality of life.[6]

And then he strikes a happy note, saying:

> He (God) has not prevented you from repenting if you do any thing bad, has not been hasty in punishing you, does not taunt you for having recourse to Him, does not disgrace you when you expose yourself to disgrace, is not relentless in accepting your repentance, does not hold you to task for committing a crime and does not disappoint you of His mercy. On the other hand, He has made even your abstinence from sin an act of virtue for you and counts your one single act of evil as only one and reckons your one virtuous act as tenfold.[7]

Again and again 'Ali reminds us of the fact, as indeed repeatedly emphasized by the Qur'an, that the world and worldly life is, by its very nature transient. And then he makes his deep spiritual and psychological contribution to the problem of man: the reason that man suffers under the transient things that pass is that he clings to the transient, he craves for things that "pass away," thus forgetting his ultimate end, the ideal, the reality, God. 'Ali thus makes craving the source of suffering and freedom from craving the source of liberation. Of freedom from craving comes peace in man and between men. Freedom from desires is an undertone of wisdom that runs through spiritual vision. 'Ali wants us to feel a sense of urgency in the solution of our spiritual problems and for us to use both reason and revelation for the solution of moral problems. He makes full use of history as a record of past nations and what happened to them, good or ill as a result of their deeds.

'Ali advises us to develop the necessary qualities of friendliness, goodwill, benevolence, love and loving kindness to all; compassion, pity, sorrow for the sufferings of all; joy in the good of all; and forgiveness, overlooking the faults of all. Then he describes other components of a *meaningful* moral life, without which a man cannot claim perfect morality. These are: the right determination, the right words on the right occasion, right action, right means of supporting one's life or right livelihood and right efforts which means to him right tensions and right relaxation. These traits cannot be achieved, as has been pointed out above, without firm belief in God, the example of the prophets and the Prophet of Islam, the expectation of the imminent end of the world and without devaluing the material world.

With this we must now conclude our comments on the testament, leaving it to the reader to analyze for themself. But before we present the text of the testament, two things ought to be mentioned briefly: namely, the circumstances in which 'Ali wrote it and secondly, the source of the text as it has reached us.

'Ali wrote this memorable document at a place called Hadirayn[8] or Hadirin while he was returning from the inconclusive battle of Siffin in 657 A.D. (37 A.H.). As has been pointed out earlier, 'Ali lived with the Prophet from the age of five or so and grew up under his personal care, embraced Islam at the age of ten (or at the most thirteen), remained the most devoted and zealous supporter of the Prophet from the first day of his call till his death[9] and participated with him enthusiastically in molding the community in the Islamic way of life and morality. After the death of the Prophet, he selflessly continued his work to preserve the heritage left behind by his great teacher. Twenty five years after the death of the Prophet, when he was called upon to lead the community as Caliph, he found Arab society going back to its pre-Islamic way of life. The principles of humanitarianism, egalitarianism, economic justice, social justice, moral values and the virtuous conduct of life taught by the Qur'an, exemplified by the Prophet and so zealously propagated by him were being forgotten by a great number of Muslims, instead indulging in luxury and material pursuits. Not only was his authority as the Caliph challenged, but he saw that conservative and reactionary forces were united to reassert themselves and to destroy the new moral order introduced by Islam. 'Ali tried his best with all the peaceful means at his command to persuade his opponents to come back to what was taught to them for so many years, but all in vain. At last the champion of peace and love had to fight[10] for the restoration and reestablishment of the Islamic way of life and morality. There too he met with treachery and rebellion from both within and without and his life-long ideals were totally frustrated. It is difficult to imagine or fully realize the agonizing, heartbreaking pain and sorrow of one who ceaselessly worked for almost sixty years of his life for an ideal and then saw with his own eyes that very ideal being destroyed. That anguish made 'Ali cry; and that cry is the *testament* being presented here. Thus the entire testament from beginning to end, is so filled with unparalleled sorrow, expressions of the sad realities of life, emotion and disheartening experiences that for a moment, he appears to have given in to pessimism. That is not so. These are cries of the soul with which 'Ali calls Muslims back to Islamic ideals of morality and conduct.

As for the source of the testament, it is taken from the famous collection of 'Ali's speeches, sermons, maxims, testaments and letters, known as the *Nahj al-Balagha*, which has been introduced in detail earlier in this volume. For the Arabic text of the testament, like the other two letters given above, Shaykh Muhammad Abduh's edition of the *Nahj al-Balagha* is used.[11]

II. Introductory note by Sharif al-Radi:

> From a testament of 'Ali ibn Abi Talib, (peace be upon him), which he wrote for his son, al-Hasan while on his way back from Siffin.

From a father, exhausted and worn-out, who acknowledges the ravages of Time,[12] is grown old, who has surrendered himself to fate (literally Time[13]) who blames (this treacherous) world,[14] who dwells in the abode of the dead,[15] and who is going to depart from this world shortly (lit. tomorrow), to his son, who (being young and inexperienced and exposed to the charms and guiles of worldly life) expects what is unattainable,[16] treads the path of those who have perished, is a target of diseases, is in the grip of the calamities and misfortunes of time (lit. a subject to the days),[17] a butt for disasters, a captive of worldly demands (lit. a slave of the world),[18] a trader in vanities, a debtor of death and its prisoner, an ally of anxieties and a companion of sorrows, a shooting mark for sudden calamities, a victim of his desires and a successor of the dead.

> [This opening paragraph of 'Ali's testament, translated above, comprising small phrases of two or three words each, is so rich in meaning and so charged with sorrow, expressions of the sadness of life, the frustration of hope and lofty ideals and the treacherous nature of this ever-changing world and its vicissitudes, that it is nearly impossible to capture its spirit in a translation, especially. It is like a small poem full of pathos and sorrow coming from the depths of the poet's heart and going straight into the heart of the reader. In these few phrases, one may find the essence of one's experience of life from the childhood to the grave. However it is not al-Hasan who is personally meant here but he is addressed only as a symbol to inexperienced young people deceived by the false temptations of this world.]

Now turning to our topic: What has become manifestly clear to me from the recession of the world from me, the restiveness of time and the advance of the Hereafter towards me (the approach of death) was sufficient enough to prevent me from thinking of any one else besides my own self, or feeling concerned about anything other than mineself (lit. what is beyond me). (And indeed, even in this state of dejection) when my anxiety about my own self monopolized me to the exclusion of any concern for others, my judgment remained truthful to me;[19] it turned me away from my (personal) desires, disclosed to me my real situation (i.e. helplessness) and (ultimately) led me to an earnestness in which there is no frivolity and to a truth which is untainted by falsehood. (While thus occupied, my thoughts turned to you and) I found you to be a part of myself, rather the whole of myself[20] so that if anything hits you, it hits me and as if when death comes to you, it comes to me. And so I became concerned about your affairs as I had been with my own and wrote to you this testament of mine seeking consolation from it, whether I live or die.

I advise you, O my son! To fear God and to stick to His commands, to fill up your heart with His remembrance and to clutch firmly at His rope;[21] for which link or connection is more trustworthy than the link between you and (your) God, if you clasp it?

Revive your heart (i.e. self) with admonition and kill it (i.e. its inordinate desires) by piety and abstinence,[22] strengthen it with firm and unwavering belief (*yaqin*)[23] and brighten it up with wisdom (*hikma*),[24] subjugate it by the (constant) remembrance of death and make it acknowledge the mortality of life (lit. prepare it for destruction), make it see the disappointments of the world and warn it of the onslaught of Time[25] and the mischief of the vicissitudes of the nights and days (*al-layali wa'layyam*).[26] Expose your heart to the account (lit. news) of past generations and remind it what befell those of the early peoples who lived before you. Travel in their (ruined) dwellings and among their vestiges and see wherein they worked and where from they departed and where they halted and alighted. You will find that they moved away (i.e. parted company with and disappeared) from their dear and near ones and settled down in a strange and solitary abode (i.e. grave). It will appear to you as if you would soon become like one of them. So be prepared and set aright for your permanent abode, do not sell the life Hereafter for the worldly life and give up talking about what you do not know or speaking about what has not been imposed upon you.[27] Restrain yourself from a path wherein you fear going astray, for desisting at the time of misguided bewildering is better than embarking on frightful courses.[28]

Enjoin upon the people to do good and be one of those who perform good deeds (and thus are counted among the most virtuous of men). Denounce what is evil with your hands and tongue (i.e. by your deeds and words).[29] Keep aloof as best as you can from him who commits evil and strive,[30] as one should strive, in the path of God, not taking to heart the reproach of any reviler.

Plunge into deep waters (i.e. face any hardship however trying it is) for the sake of truth wherever it may be; acquire a deep and penetrating knowledge of religion; accustom yourself to be patient under unpleasant circumstances. Indeed, the best trait is patience for the sake of Truth (al-haqq).

Seek for yourself the protection of your God in all your concerns, for you would thus be making it (self) resort to a safe and well-protected shelter and a powerful defender.

Whatever be your wants ask only from your Lord, for to give or to bestow as well as to withhold or to refuse lie only in His power (lit. hand); and keep on seeking His blessings and guidance.[31] Try to understand my advice, not allowing yourself to ignore it, for the best advice (lit. words) are those that benefit (the listener). Remember that there is no good in a knowledge which does not benefit and that one cannot derive any profit from knowledge which is not worth acquiring.

O my son, when I saw that I have become old and also noticed that my weakness (due to age) is increasing, I hastened to make this 'will' to you and have mentioned some of its points lest my end may come before I have imparted to you what is in my mind, or my mental capacities (lit. judgment) may decline as I have declined in body. Or else before my advice reaches you, you may be overpowered by passion and worldly temptations and may become like a stubborn, intractable horse.[32]

The heart of a youth is like fertile land; it grows whatever seeds are cast into it.[33] I have, therefore, made haste to educate you, before your heart becomes too hard and your mind becomes too engrossed, so that you may acquire by the efforts of your own judgment some thing whose search and experience have been vouchsafed to you by men of experience. My advice would save you from seeking help from others and relieve you from the struggle of gaining experience (i.e. from going through the process of trial and error); and there may thus come to you what we have been trying to acquire and there may dawn upon you what was for us frequently in the dark.

O my son, although I have not been granted a long life like those who were before me, yet I have looked into their works, have pondered over their history and have traveled among their ruins and remains, till I became like one of them; nay, I have rather lived since the time of the first of them to that of the last of them and thus I have acquired an insight into their affairs (i.e. I have pondered over their lives, deeds and history so deep that I now feel as if I have lived and worked with them from the dawn of history down to our own times). I have thus recognized what was pure (good) in them and what was turbid, what was profitable and what was harmful (i.e. what did them good and what brought them harm and destruction). I have selected for you from the store (of my experience and knowledge) its best part[34] and have reserved for you the most becoming portion of it, keeping away from you what was ignoble or unbecoming therein. And I felt, when I was concerned about you as an affectionate father is (always) concerned and had made up my mind to educate you, that this should be done when you are yet of tender age and in the prime of your life and still have guileless (honest) and sincere intentions and a pure and unadulterated mind.

Originally I wanted to teach you first (of all) the Book of God and its interpretation, the laws of Islam and its ordinances and what is lawful (*halal*) in it and what is unlawful (*haraatri*) and for the time being not to touch any other subject (lit. not going beyond this to any thing else). But I feared you may become confused by what the people differ about due to their various inclinations and opinions, just as they themselves have been confused and so, in spite of the fact that I dislike to admonish you, I found it more desirable to explain all this firmly to you instead of letting you submit to something due to which you may not be safe from destruction. And I hope that God would enable you to do the correct thing and would guide you to the right path. It was for this reason that I have made to you this 'will' of mine.

And know, O my son, the dearest to me of what you can learn from my testament are to fear God (*Taqwa*[35]), to concentrate on and to confine your self to what has been prescribed by Him and to adopt the course followed by your ancestors[36] and the virtuous ones from among your family members. They had (already) examined for themselves what you can examine (now) and they had (thoroughly) deliberated on what you can deliberate (now), but in the end they themselves were compelled to adopt only what they found to be the best and to abstain from what appeared to them to be unnecessary for themselves. So if your mind refuses to accept this (i.e. the findings of your predecessors) without making your own investigations as they did theirs, let then your search for it be by means of strenuous understanding and learning and not by plunging into doubts and getting entangled in controversies.

Before looking into that, (i.e. before you start thinking and deliberating over controversial problems) begin by seeking help from your Lord and desiring His guidance, shaking aside every misgiving which casts you into doubt or hands you over to misguidance. When you feel sure that your heart is pure and humble (i.e. your mind is clear and receptive) and your judgment is perfect and unshaky and that your concern about the problem is the only concern, (i.e. has become your real desire to search for truth) only then look into what I have explained to you. But if you are unable to collect your mental faculties and employ your study and thought as you expect from yourself, you should realize that you are merely stumbling like a weak-sighted she-camel and plunging into the dark night, while the seeker of Truth (*din*)[37] is not one who stumbles or gets confused. And abstention from this (confusion, doubt or skepticism) is the best (course).

So understand my advice, O my son; and know that the master of death is also the master of life, that the one who is the creator is also the annihilator, the one who is annihilator is also the restorer, the one who is inflictor (of calamities) is also the savior and that the world is not going to last forever with its happiness and tribulations destined for it by God and that the requital would come in the next life or other such things of which you have no knowledge. If any of these things seem to be difficult to you, attribute this to your ignorance of it, for you were first created ignorant and then you were taught. There is many a thing (in this mysterious world) of which you are ignorant, in which your judgment is bewildered and your sight is confounded and yet afterwards (i.e. gradually) you start perceiving things in their true perspective. So take refuge and cling to Him who has created you, nourished you and made you of harmonious build; and let your worship be for Him alone, towards Him are your desires and from Him springs your fear.

And know, my son, that no one taught (lit. informed) us about God (i.e. has taught mankind in such a great detail about the concept of God in itself and in relation to mankind) as did the Prophet, peace be upon him and his family members. Be then content[38] with him as a leader and a guide towards salvation. I have not fallen short in giving you (my) sincere advice and (remember) you shall never reach in your consideration for your own welfare the extent of my contemplations for it, however hard you may try to do so.[39]

And know, my son, that had there been a partner to your Lord, his messengers would have surely come to you, you would have seen the signs of his kingdom[40] and power and would have known his acts and attributes. But He is the one God, as He has Himself described Himself. No one opposes Him in His sovereignty (or supreme authority, kingdom) and He shall remain always and has remained always (i.e. has never been and shall never be opposed in His supreme authority). He is the First before all things without any beginning and the Last of all things without any end.[41]

When you have known this do what one like yourself should do in this insignificant position, in the smallness of his power, in the greatness of his helplessness and in his dire need of his Lord, in seeking obedience to Him, fearing His punishment and being afraid of His displeasure, for He has not commanded you to do but what is good and has not forbidden you to do except what is bad.

O my son, I have explained to you about this world and its (ever-changing) condition, its ephemeral, evanescent, declining, transitional, changing and momentary nature. I have likewise told you about the next world and what has been prepared for the people there and have quoted for you examples about both of them (the world here and the hereafter) so that you may take a lesson from them and try to equip yourself (for both the worlds).

The example of those who have been able to test and understand this world is like a party of travelers who have found it (this world) a drought stricken and worthless halting place and they have thus to proceed looking forward to a fertile land and a spot overgrown with vegetation and greenery. They therefore bear up with the difficulties of separation from their friends, the roughness of the journey and the coarseness of their food in order that they may reach their comfortable abode and the place where they could settle down (nicely). They do not feel any pain from all these (difficulties) and do not consider the expenses incurred for the purpose to have been wasted. Nothing is dearer to them than what brings them near their alighting place (destination) and makes them approach their chosen abode.

And the example of those who have become deluded by this world is like that of a people who were in a fertile place but left it for a drought-stricken and inhospitable one. Nothing could then be more distasteful and hateful to them than what they had done to themselves by leaving (the most fertile and pleasant) place they were in, for that whereto they had rashly traveled and had come to an arid and barren place.

O my son! make your own self a 'balance' (*mizan*) between yourself and others and like for others what you like for yourself and dislike for them what you dislike for yourself. Do not be unjust (to others), just as you would not like to be treated unjustly and do kindness (to others) as you would like kindness to be done to yourself.[42] Consider that thing to be bad for your own self which you consider to be bad for others and be pleased with men with what you are pleased with from yourself. Do not say what you do not know, or even if you know it is not sufficient enough. And do not say what you would not like to be said to you.

And know that vanity is the antithesis of rectitude and the bane of intellect. Strive to work hard and do not be merely a 'treasurer' for others (i.e. you accumulate wealth for others to spend after you leave it behind); and when you have been guided to the right path, be as humble as you can before your Lord.

And know that there lies in front of you a long and distant road and hard labor and that you cannot depend on it with good scouting and provisions that may suffice for your needs, together with as little weight on you as possible (lit. with a 'light back'). So do not carry on your back anything beyond your strength (i.e. do not nourish so many ambitions, nor take upon yourself responsibilities and desires that you cannot fulfill) lest the weight of it become a burden on you. And when you find a starving or needy person who can carry your provisions for the Day of Resurrection and may deliver these (provisions) to you tomorrow (i.e. the Day of Resurrection) when you would need them, consider him to be a Godsend and allow him to carry them away (i.e. distribute your wealth amongst the destitute and needy persons and thus lighten your burden). Provide him amply while he is with you, for perhaps you may later on search for him and may not find him.

And consider him God-sent who borrows from you while you are rich so that he may pay you back at the time of your adversity.

And know that you have before you a difficult mountain pass[43] (traveling through) which he who has a light load is in a better position than he who is heavily loaded and the slow traveler is worse off than a swift one and that you would descend through that pass either into Paradise or into Hell; and so employ a scout (i.e. make your guide your good deeds and virtuous acts) for yourself before you descend and prepare the dwelling-place before you alight, for after death there will not be any occasion for repentance and no possibility of a return to this world.

And know that He who possesses the treasures of the earth and the skies has given you freedom to pray and has undertaken to answer (your prayers).[44] He has ordered you to beg from Him so that He may give to you[45] and to ask for His mercy so that He may be merciful to you.[46] He has not put between you and Himself any one who may screen you from Him and has not compelled you to resort to any one who may intercede with Him for you. He has not prevented you from repenting if you do anything wrong,[47] has not been hasty in punishing you, does not taunt you for having recourse to Him, does not disgrace you when you expose yourself to disgrace, is not hesitant in accepting your repentance, does not take you to task for committing a crime and does not disappoint you of His mercy. On the other hand, He has made even your abstinence from sin an act of virtue for you and counts your one single act of evil as only one and reckons your one virtuous act as ten-fold.[48] He has opened for you the door of repentance and atonement, so that when you call Him, He hears your call and when you commune with Him secretly, He knows what your intimate talk means (i.e. what is in your heart). You then lay before Him your needs, disclose to Him what is in your mind, complain to Him of your anxieties, beg Him to dispel your worries, request Him to help you in your difficulties (lit. affairs) and ask Him to bestow on you such treasures of His mercy as none else has the power to give, namely an increase in life, physical health and abundance of livelihood.

Then, He has placed in your hands the keys of His treasures by permitting you to beg from Him, so that whenever you so desire you can open the doors of His blessing by prayer and can make the showers of His mercy rain upon you. You should never become despondent if there is a delay in His response, for a gift is according to one's intention. It is possible that He may delay His response in order that the reward of the beggar may increase thereby and the gift of the expectant may become larger. Sometimes you ask for a thing but it is not given to you and you are given something better than what you had asked, either immediately or after some time; or it is kept away from you for the sake of something which is better for you, for there is many a thing requested by you in which lies the destruction of your faith if it is given to you. Let your request, therefore, be for a thing the beauty of which remains for you and the baneful effect of which is dispelled from you. As to wealth, it would not endure, nor would it last for long.

And know that you have been created merely for the next world, not for this one; for perishing, not for lasting; and for death, not for life; that you are in a station of departure and in a home (meant) for stocking provisions and that you are marching on the road to the next world; that you are being chased by death from which none who flees escapes and which is not missed by any one who seeks it; so that it is inevitable that it should overtake man. So remain cautious of it lest it may come to you while you are in a bad condition of which you had been thinking of repenting and it may intervene between you and your intention, causing thereby the destruction of your soul.

O my son, think of death most of your time as also of that which you would have to come upon and arrive at after your death, so that it (death) may come to you when you have already taken due precaution against it and have girded up your loins to meet it and it may not thus come to you suddenly and overpower you.

Beware of being deceived by the attachment of worldly people to the world and their extreme fondness for it; for God has clearly told you the truth about (the nature and character of) this world, and also the world itself has described its own self to you, disclosing its mortal characters[49] and its faults and weaknesses. These worldly people are merely barking dogs and carnivorous wild beasts, growling at each other, the powerful devouring the weaker, the bigger dominating the smaller. Some of them (worldly people) are like tethered cattle (i.e. they have lost their sense of judgment and freedom of thought and are prisoners of their ambitions, desires and carnal pleasures), while others are free who have lost (shed) their tethers and have betaken themselves to an unknown path (i.e. whom wealth and power have made like unruly beasts trampling, crushing and killing their fellows. They have lost balance in their mind, not knowing what they are doing and where they are going).

These (worldly people) are like flocks of camels browsing calamities and distress in a difficult and uneven valley, having no camel-herd to guard them and no grazier to make them graze. The world has led them to the path of blindness and has snatched away their eyes from the lamppost of guidance (i.e. from the divine light) and so they have strayed away in its (world's) bewilderment and have become submerged in its luxuries. They have made the world their Mammon; the world has (consequently) played with them and they have played with it, forgetting what lies beyond.

Wait a bit! The darkness would be dispelled, as if the caravan (of life) has already arrived (at its destination) and he who hastens is about to join it.

And know my son that he who rides the night and the day, (i.e. Time) is made to travel (i.e. move onward), although he may feel himself standing and indeed traverses the distance, even though he may be stationary and motionless (i.e. every day is carrying him a step farther in his journey towards death and thus man is destined to proceed to his final destination).

And know for certain that you shall never realize your hopes and shall never escape your end and that you are treading the same path as did those before you. So be modest in your demand, earn your livelihood in a becoming manner, for there is many a demand which drags one to complete loss and disappointment (lit. leads to war: al-harb), for every seeker (i.e. greedy person) is not given what he seeks and every good and modest person is not denied his due.

Keep yourself away from every meanness, even though it may drive you towards desirable objects, because you shall never find a substitute for having degraded yourself. Be not a slave to any other person when God has made you a free man; what is the benefit of a good thing which can be achieved only by doing something evil, or of prosperity which cannot be attained except through adversity?

Beware, lest the dromedaries of greed may gallop away with you and bring you to the springs of destruction. If you can afford not to have any benefactor between yourself and God, do so, for you are doing (in any case) to get your due and take your share. And a little from God, the Glorious, is greater and nobler than much from His creatures—although everything really comes from Him alone.

It is easier to make amends for what you lose by remaining silent than for what you lose by speaking out. (Remember) the presentation of what is there in a water-skin is by tying up its mouth firmly and the guarding of what there is in your hands is dearer to me than your seeking what is in the hands (i.e. possession) of someone else[50] and the bitterness of despair is better than begging from others.

Poverty with chastity is better than richness with debauchery[51] (i.e. sin or immorality). Remember a man can guard his secrets best himself (i.e. nobody can guard your secrets better than you).

There are people who try their best to acquire something which is the most harmful to them (lit. there is many a striver after what is harmful to him).

He who talks too much, drivels and he who ponders, gains insight.

Associate with the virtuous that you may become one of them and stay away from the wicked that you may be distinguished from them (i.e. you will abstain from wickedness).

The worst food is the unlawful one[52] (i.e. livelihood acquired by foul means is the worst form of livelihood).

Cruelty or oppression to a weak person is the worst form of crime.

When kindness produces cruel results then cruelty is the real kindness; very often a medicine proves to be a malady and a malady to be a medicine; and often an insincere person gives a sincere advice while he from whom sincerity is expected proves deceitful.

Beware of placing your reliance on vain desires, for they are the merchandise of fools. Wisdom lies in guarding your experienceand the best of what you have experienced is what admonishes you.

Hasten to avail of an opportunity before it becomes barred up. Every seeker does not attain his object and everyone missing does not come back. It is an evil thing to waste one's provisions and spoil the life of the hereafter. Every thing has an end and what has been destined for you, shall soon be delivered to you.

The trader has to take a risk and many a small thing grows more vigorously than a large one.

There is no good in a contemptible helper or a suspect friend.

Take the dromedary of Time easy as long as its young[53] is obedient to you (i.e. as long as Time is favorably disposed to you).

Do not take unnecessary risk for the desire of some thing greater than what you have (i.e. do not endanger yourself for unreasonable and extravagant hopes).

Beware lest (due to your ambitions) you may be confronted with quarrels and enmities.

Persuade yourself to be friend to your brother (i.e. friend) when he cuts you off (i.e. severs friendly relations with you), to be mild and conciliating when he is niggardly in his gift (of help), to approach him when he stays away from you, to be soft when he is hard, to forgive when he commits a crime, so that it may appear that (he is your master and) you are a slave of his and as if he is your benefactor. But be careful not to do all this where it is not desirable; neither towards one who does not deserve it.[54]

Do not take the enemy of your friend to be your friend lest you antagonize your friend. Be sincere in your advice to your brother, whether it is good or bad and swallow up your anger, for I have not seen any draught sweeter than it in its result (taste), or more delicious in its aftermath. Be soft to him who treats you with haughtiness, for he may soon soften towards you.[55] Conquer your enemy by kindness for this is the sweeter of the two victories. When you intend to dissociate from your brother let there remain some link with you, so that he may return to you on any day if he so desires. Confirm the opinion of one who thinks well of you (i.e. prove yourself worthy of the good opinion which some one holds of you and do not disappoint him by behaving in a different manner).

Do not ignore the due of your brother relying on the relationship between you and him, for he will not remain your friend (lit. brother) if his rights are slighted or ignored by you.

Let not your close relatives (i.e. members of your household) be the most unfortunate people on account of you (i.e. because of your bad temper and ill-treatment of them).

Do not run after him who tries to ignore you. You should never allow your friend (lit. brother) to become stronger than you in cutting you off (in your relationship), in safeguarding his kinship with you (i.e.

the enmity of your brother should not overcome the consideration and friendship you should show towards him, or his ill-treatment of you should not overpower (your kind treatment of) him.

You should never be quicker to ill-treat others than you are to treat them well and do not make much of the injustice of one who is unjust to you, for he is (in fact) striving to injure himself and thus to benefit you; and the requital of one who pleases you is not that you displease him.

And know my son that livelihood is of two sorts: a livelihood which you seek and another livelihood which seeks you, so that if you do not go to it, it comes to you itself.

How unbecoming (painful) is humiliation at the time of need and callousness when one is rich.

What belongs to you of this world is that with which you can improve your position (in this world and hereafter) and if you worry about what has slipped out of your hands, then worry also about what has not reached you.

Draw your conclusions (or make comparisons) about what has not happened with what has happened to you, for things are often alike. Be not one of those whom admonition does no good except when you torture him excessively, because a wise man is admonished by training or education while animals are not corrected (made docile) except by beating.

Discard from yourself crowding anxieties by patient resolve and the goodness or firmness of belief.[56]

He who leaves the middle course goes astray.

A companion is to be treated like a kinsman and a sincere friend is he who is sincere in absence (i.e. speaks well of you even behind your back).

Passion is the partner of blindness[57] (i.e. inordinate and carnal desires are like blindness which may lead a person to destruction and calamity).

There is many a near one who is further away than a distant one, while there is many a distant one who is nearer than a near one and a stranger is he who does not have a beloved one.

He who transgresses the truth finds his path to be narrow and he who confines himself to his position (i.e. remains within his limits) retains it longer.

The most reliable link which you can grasp is the link between you and God,[58] the Glorious.

He who does not care for you is your enemy.

When achievement of an object (i.e. ambition or desire) leads to destruction, its renunciation is the real achievement.[59]

Every defect (of your enemy) is not revealed (to you) and every opportunity is not availed of. Very often a man (gifted with) sight (i.e. wise or having insight and knowledge) misses his object while a blind one (i.e. uneducated or foolish) finds the right course.

Put off what is evil, for you can hasten it (i.e. get it) whenever you like. To sever connections with an ignorant man establishes friendship with a wise person.

He who feels secure from (the ravages of) Time is betrayed by it and he who honors it (i.e. exalts its importance) is disgraced by it.

Every one who shoots does not hit the target (i.e. it is not always necessary that one should succeed in one's hopes or desires).

When the ruler changes, Time also changes (i.e. living conditions and circumstances).

Make sure (lit. ask or investigate) about your companion before embarking on a journey and (find out) about the neighbor before adopting a place as your home.

Beware of indulging in a speech which is ludicrous, even though you speak on the authority of someone else.

Beware of showing jealousy when there is no occasion for it, for this would lead a healthy one towards disease and an innocent one towards suspicion (sin).

Assign to each one of your servants a job for which you hold him responsible, for it is more appropriate that they do not entrust their jobs to one another (i.e. do not shift their responsibility).

Honor your family members, for they are the wings with which you fly and are the origin towards which you return as well as they are your hands with which you attack (i.e. fight your enemy).

I entrust to God your faith and your world and I beg Him the best dispensation concerning your present and your future, your life in this world and the life Hereafter.

Notes and References
Chapter Six

1. Laurence Collier, *Flight From Conflict*, London 1947, p. 51

2. E.E. Kellett, *A short History of Religion*, London 1939, p. 3.

3. The Qur'an, 33:21.

4. Though not of our direct concern here, it is of academic inter-

est to note that this very fact, unfortunately for the history of religions, has often been the root cause of internal splits and sectarian divisions within the framework of major religious traditions; for example, the schools of Mahayana and Theravada in Buddhism, Shaivite and Vaishnavite in Hinduism and the Catholic and Orthodox, as well as many other Churches, in Christianity. Islam was no exception.

5. Al-Hasan, the elder son of 'Ali and Fatima, was born in 624-5 A.D. (3 A.H.). He was ardently loved by his grandfather, the Prophet, to whom he is reported to have resembled in appearance. He was acclaimed as caliph by the Kufans in 660 A.D. (41 A.H.) soon after 'Ali's death, but abdicated in favor of Mu'awiya only after a few months, and lived a quiet life in Medina until his death in 669 A.D. (49 A.H.). For a detailed account of his abdication and life see H.M. Jafri, *Origins and Early Development of Shi'a Islam*, London 1979, pp. 130-173.

6. See the text of the testament below.

7. *Ibid.*

8. Al-Hadir, literally means a cultivated district or a settlement on the outskirts of a large city where people stop and take up their abode by a source of water. Here according to one version it refers to the district in the vicinity of Aleppo (Halab). Why it is used in the dual form is thus explained that after the conquest of Qinnisrin, its inhabitants came and settled down in this township. According to Muhammad Abduh, it was known in the plural form, Hadirin and was a township inhabited by different tribes located in the vicinity of the plain of Siffin where the battle between 'Ali and Mu'awiya was fought in 657 A.D. (37 A.H.). After his return from Siffin, 'Ali alighted at this place. See al-Baladhuri, *Kitab al-Futuh al-Buldan*, English Tr. P.K. Hitti, *The Origins of the Islamic State*, reprint Beirut 1966, pp. 224 f; Yaqut, *Mu'jam al-Buldan*, ed. Wustenfeld, Leipzig 1867, II, pp. 184 ff,

Shaykh M. 'Abduh, *Nahj al-Balagha*, Cairo, n.d., p.307, footnote 2.

9. For details and original sources see S.H.M. Jafri, loc. cit., pp. 17ff.

10. Jafri, loc. cit., pp. 90 ff.

11. Shaykh Abduh's edition has run through many editions so far; the one I am using is published by the Dar al-Sha'b, Cairo n.d. and is revised by Muhammad Ahmad 'Ashur and Muhammad Ibrahim al-Banna.

12. *Al-muqir li'l-zaman.* *Zaman* is one of several words in Arabic used for time. For its employed meaning see footnote 13 below where its synonym *dahir* is explained.

13. *Dahir* and its synonym *zaman* above in footnote 12 mean time but it is frequently used in the meaning of destiny, calamities and misfortunes which time brings with it.

14. *Al-dham* literally means a vice, fault, defect or the like (see Lane: 977), *al-dham li'l dunya* however, signifies treacherous character of the world, which 'Ali blames.

15. The Qur'an, 14:45–"*And you dwelt in the dwellings of men who wronged themselves.*"

16. Wishes to have an everlasting and peaceful life which no one was able to attain.

17. *Rahina wa rahinaht al-ayyam* lit. means pawn, pledged or something mortgaged. *Ayyam*, which lit. means days, is often used in Arabic poetry as a synonym for time and signifies an agent of misfortunes, causing perpetual change which brings ruin and destruction.

18. *'Abd al-dunya* and all the other eight phrases which follow refer

to the inherent nature of man as such and not to al-Hasan as an individual.

19. *Fasaddaqani ra'i*, lit. 'my judgment was, or proved, true' (Lane, 1667) here means that in spite of all the frustrations and anxieties about what happened in Siffin and other worldly affairs, I remembered God and put all my trust in Him alone.

20. Being my son you are my body and soul and whenever I look at you I feel as if I look at myself. For such expressions see many verses from pre-Islamic Arabic poetry quoted by Ibn Abi'l-Hadid, *Sharh*, vol. XVI, pp. 61f.

21. cf. The Qur'an, 3:103–"*And hold fast to the rope of God all together and do not be divided.*"

22. *Zuhhaduhu* and *zuhd*, to devote oneself to God in such a way as to abstain from worldly pleasures and material involvement, or to be free from worldly desires and temptations, hence *zuhd* which is used for asceticism and which ultimately developed into Sufism.

23. *Yaqin*, lit. conviction, is one of the basic terminologies used in Islam, signifying firm and unwavering faith and belief, hence *'ilm al-yaqin* as in 102:5, "*…Nay, you would know with firm knowledge*", and *haqq al-yaqin* as in 69:51, "*and verily it is the Truth of assured certainty*"; and *'ayn al-yaqin* as in 102:7, "*again, you shall see it with certainty of sight.*"

24. cf. The Qur'an, 2:269–"*And he to whom wisdom is granted receives, indeed, a benefit overflowing.*"

25. *Dahr* see footnote 13 above.

26. *Al-layali wa'l ayyam*, literally nights and days is used in Arabic for changing time and the calamities it brings to mankind. See

footnote 17 above.

27. Do not speculate and pass judgment over subjects about which you are not in a position to form an opinion; also, it is not incumbent on you to speak and give your opinion.

28. *Rukub al-ahwal*, lit. means to go on a voyage on a rough (swollen) sea or to embark upon danger. Here it signifies taking the path of uncertainties, dangers and unforeseen risks.

29. The principle of *al-amr bi'l ma'ruf wa naha 'an al-munkar* which is one of the five fundamental principles (*usul al-Khamsa*) was, perhaps, adopted by both the Mu'tazilites and the Shi'ites from these words of 'Ali in the testament *wa amr bi'l ma'ruf takun min ahlihi wa ankar al-munkar bi yadika wa lisanika.*

30. *Jihad*, one of the fundamental teachings of Islam literally means to strive for; it may, in a certain situation, and in most extraordinary circumstances require fighting in the cause of God as a form of self-sacrifice. But its essence, *jihad* consists of (1) a true and sincere faith in God (2) an earnest and ceaseless activity, involving sacrifice of all sorts: self, person or property in the service of God and therefore humanity. The greatest *Jihad* is that which one carries out against ones own self.

31. *Wa akthana al-istikhara. Istikhara* here does not mean divination as it was commonly practiced by the Arabs before Islam. Here it means to ask God's guidance and permission before embarking upon an undertaking and in this sense it has universally been in practice among the Muslims. See *Encyclopaedia of Islam* (2nd ed.), article "Istikhara"; Ibn Abi'l-Hadid, *Sharh* vol. XVI. p. 65.

32. *Al-sa'ab-in al-nufur. Nafur* or *nufur* is used for a she-camel or horse which is untrained and therefore difficult. Here it means that if a young man is left alone without guidance he may become a prey to desires and temptations to the extent that nothing could

influence his personality. This idea is further explained in the following paragraph of the testament.

33. Allowing things sown in it to grow verdantly and to produce luxuriously.

34. In 'Abduh's edition it reads *wa min kull-i amr-in nakhila* means *al-mukhtar al-mustafa*, the "best choice or the best selection," but in Abul Fadl Ibrahim's and in Ibn Abi 'l-Hadid's it reads *min kull-i amr-in jalila*, "from every thing of great importance."

35. *Taqwa*, a key word in the Qur'anic concept of morality and religious consciousness is commonly translated as "the fear of God," but in fact its comprehensiveness in meaning and sense can hardly be rendered into English. It is an attitude denoting restraint or guarding one's tongue, hand and heart from evil, hence righteousness, piety and good conduct.

36. *Al-awwaluna min aba'ika*, most probably refer to Hashim b. 'Abd al-Manaf, 'Abd al-Muttalib and Abu Talib. It may also refer to the earliest immigrants from among the Banu Hashim and Banu Muttalib. see, *Hadid*, vol. XVI, p. 71.

37. The term *din* is the most comprehensive of all the terms used in Islamic-Qur'anic vocabulary to describe a meaningful life. It can be translated in different ways according to the context. Here 'truth' is the best rendering.

38. *Farad bihi ra'id-an*, "to be content with him" means to accept his teachings wholeheartedly and with firm faith and not to wander about seeking truth elsewhere.

39. It refers to the preceding sentence that you can never find a better leader, guide and perfect teacher than the Prophet of God, nor better guidance than that given by him.

40. *Fi mulkihi 'ahad-un*, cf. *lahu mulk al-samawat wa'l ard*, "To Him

belongs the Kingdom or domain of the heavens and the earth" (The Qur'an, 57:2).

41. cf. The Qur'an 57:3–"*He is the First and the Last, the Evident and the Immanent.*" The "First without any beginning" and "the Last without any end" negate any relativity with which 'firstness' or 'endness' is understood in human vocabulary.

42. cf. The Qur'an, 28:77–"*Be kind to others as God has been kind to you.*"
43. *'Aqba-tun ka'ud-an.* *'Aqba* means a steep road or a track, pass or a mountain-road, while *Ka'ud* means most difficult or insurmountable obstacle; perhaps it refers to the journey from Here to the Hereafter or from this worldly life to the Day of Judgment.

44. cf. The Qur'an, 40:60–"*And your Lord says: call on Me and I will answer your prayer.*"

45. cf. The Qur'an, 4:32–"*Ask God for His bounty.*"

46. cf. The Qur'an, 8:33–"*...and God was not going to punish them while they could ask for pardon.*"

47. cf. The Qur'an, 25:70–"*Unless he repents, believes and works righteous deeds, for God will change the evil of such persons into good, and God is oft-Forgiving, most Merciful.*"

48. cf. The Qur'an, 6:160–"*He who does a good deed shall have ten times as much of his reward (but) he who does a bad deed shall only be recompensed with the like of it, and no wrong shall be done unto them.*"

49. *Al-na'i* or *na'a*, means news of some one's death, hence mortal character. But in Abu'1-Fadl and Ibn Abi'1-Hadid, 16:89, it reads *na'at*, which would mean that the world has explained or described its own characteristics (faults and weaknesses).

50. cf. The Qur'an, 17:29—"*Make not your hand tied (like a niggard's) to your neck, nor stretch it forth to its utmost reach (i.e. spend-thrift) so that you become blameworthy and destitute.*"

51. Whatever you earn through hard but respectable labor (in a craft or profession), though with little return is better than the wealth you amass through immoral means, corruption and wickedness.

52. cf. The Qur'an, 4:10—"*Those who unjustly eat up the property of orphans, devour a fire into their own bellies; they will soon be enduring a blazing fire.*"

53. *Al-qa'ud*, sing. *qa'ada, aq'ad*, means a young camel fit for riding whenever required, it is used here metaphorically for Time or worldly affairs when they are in your control or favorable to you.

54. See many famous verses from pre-Islamic poetry to the same effect quoted by Ibn Abi'l-Hadid, in *Sharh*, vol. XVI, p. 107.

55. cf. The Qur'an, 41:34—"*Repel the evil deed with one which is better, then (understand) he between whom and you there was enmity (will become) as though he was a bosom friend.*"

56. In 'Abduh's edition it reads *atrah 'anka waridat al-humum bi 'azai'm al-sabr wa husn al-yaqin* which has been translated above, but Ibn Abi'l-Hadid points out that in some other recensions it reads: *atrah 'anka waridat al-humum bi husn al-sabr wa karam al-'aza*, which would mean "Discard from yourself the crowding anxieties by goodness of patience and with the magnanimity of accepting the loss."

57. *Wa 'l hawa sharik al-'ama*, but in the first edition of 'Abduh's it reads, *wa 'l hawa sharik al-'aza* which means misfortune, wretchedness or suffering and thus the phrase would mean "passion is the partner of misfortunes or suffering."

58. cf. The Qur'an, 2:256—"*Whoever rejects evil and believes in God has*

grasped the most trustworthy link that never breaks."

59. When man's success in his worldly and materialistic pursuits becomes so involved that it may lead him to a sinful life, then it is failure in attaining worldly objects that is his real success in life.

SELECT BIBLIOGRAPHY

The Holy Qur'an.

Nahj al-Balagha, Collection of Sermons, Letters and Maxims of Ali B. Abi Talib, Compiled by Al-Sharif al-Radi.

Editions Used:

Abdul Razzaq Malihabadi and Rais Ahmad Jafri, with Urdu tr. and commentary, Lahore, 1963.

Muhammad Abul Fadl Ibrahim, ed. 2 volumes Cairo, 1963. Dr. Subh-i Salih, ed., Beirut, 1967.

Shaykh Muhammad Abduh, with notes and glossary, ed. by Muhammad Ashur et.al, Cairo, n.d.

Abu'l Faraj al-Isfahani, *Kitab al-Aghani*, Beirut, 1973.

Abu Muhammad al-Hasan b. Shu'ba, *Tuhaf al-Uqul*, ed. Muhammad Sadiq, Tehran, 1394 AH.

Ahmad B. Hanbal, *Al-Musnad*, Cairo, 1895.

Al-Baladhuri, Ahmad b. Yahya, *Ansab al-Ashraf*, vol. i, ed. Muhammad Hamidullah, Cairo, 1955.

Arshi, Imtiyaz Ali., *Istinad-i Nahj al-Balagha*, Lucknow, 1972.

Brand, R.B., ed. *Social Justice*, N.Y., 1962.

Donohue, John, et al. ed. *Islam in Transition*, New York, 1982.

Durkheim, Emile. *Elementary Forms of Religious Life*. London, 1915.

The Encyclopedia of Modern Islamic World. New York, Oxford University Press, 1995.

Encyclopedia of Religion and Ethics. London, 1987.

Engineer, Asghar Ali. *The Islamic State*. Bombay, 1994.

Ginsberg, Morris. *On the Diversity of Morals*. London, 1967.

Glasner, Peter E. *The Sociology of Secularisation: a critique of a concept*. London, 1977.

Goldziher, Ignaz. *Muhammedanische Studien*. English tr. S.M. Stern and C.R. Berber. *Muslim Studies*. London 1967-1972.

Hobsbawm, E.G. *The Age of Revolution, 1789-1948*. New York, 1962.

Ibn Abd al-Barr. *Kitab al-Isti'ab*. Cairo, n.d.

Ibn Abd Rabbih, Ahmad b. Muhammad. *Al-Iqd al-Farid*, ed. Ahmad Am in et. al, Cairo 1952-56.

Ibn Abi'l Hadid, *Sharh Nahj al-Balagha*. ed. Muhammad Abu'l Fadl, Ibrahim, Cairo, 1959.

Ibn Asakir, Ali B. al-Hasan. *Tarikh Madinat Dimashq*. Damascus, n.d.

Ibn Durayd, Muhammad b. al-Hasan. *Kitab al-Ishtiqaq*. ed. Wustenfeld, Gottingen 1854.

Ibn Hajr al-Asqalani. *Tahdhib al-Tahdhib*. Hyderabad, 1325 AH.

Ibn Hisham. *Sirat Rasul Allah*. ed. Mustafa Saqqa et. al. Cairo, 1936.
Ibn al-Imad al-Hanbali. *Shadharat al-Dhahab*. Cairo, 1350 AH.

122

Ibn Khaldun, Abd al-Rahman. *Al-Muqaddima*. Cairo, 1322 AH.

Ibn Sa'd. *Kitab al-Tabaqat al-Kubra*, Beirut, 1957.

Ibn Tiqtaqa, Muhammad b. Ali. *Al-Fakhrifi'Adab al-Sultaniyya*. Cairo, 1951.

Iqbal, Sir Muhammad. *The Reconstruction of Religious Thought in Islam*. ed. Sheikh M. Saeed. Lahore, 1986.

Issawi, Charles. tr. *An Arab Philosophy of History: Selection from the Prolegomena of Ibn Khaldun*. London, 1950.

Jafri, S.H.M. *Origins and Early Development of Shi'a Islam*. London, 1979.

Jullundhri, Rashid Ahmad. *Islam And Current Issues*. Lahore, n.d.

Lane, E.W. *An Arabic-English Lexicon*. London, 1863.

Mas'udi, Ali b. Husayn. *Muruj al-Dhahab*. Beirut, 1966.

Al-Mawardi, Abu'l Hasan Ali B. Muhammad. *Al-Ahkam al-Sultaniyya, wa'l-wilayat al-Diniyya*. Cairo, 1960.

Mawdudi, Abu'1-AIa. *Khilafatwa Mulukiyat*. Lahore, 1966.

Al-Mubarrad, Muhammad b. Yazid. *Kitab al-Kamil*. Cairo, n.d.

Muir, Sir William. *The Caliphate: its Rise, Decline and Fall*. Beirut 1965.

Al-Najashi, Ahmad B. Ali. *Kitab al-Rijal*. Tehran, n.d.
Nasr, Seyyed Hossein. *Islamic Studies*. Beirut, 1967.

The New Encyclopedia Britannica, 15th ed. 1980.

Nicholson, R.A. *A Literary History of the Arabs.* Cambridge, 1956.

Al-Nuwayri, Shihab al-Din Ahmad. *Nihqyat al-Arab fi'l-Funun alAdab.* Cairo, 1951.

Qadi Nu'man Abu Hanifa. *Da'aim al-Islam.* ed. A.A.A. Fyzee. Cairo, 1951.

Qamaruddin Khan. *Political Concepts in the Qur'an.* Karachi, 1982.

Rahman, Fazlur. *Islam.* London, 1966.

Shah Wali Allah, Fiqh Umar. tr. Abu Yahya Imam Khan Nosahri. *Risala Dar Madhhab Faruq-e Azam.* Lahore, 1952.

Tabari, Muhammad B. Jarir. *Tarikh al-Rasul Wa'l-Muluk.* ed. M.J. De Goeje, et. al. Leiden, 1879-1901.

Al-Tusi, Muhammad b. Hasan. *Al-Fihrist.* Mashhad (Iran), n.d.

Watt, W. Montgomery. *Muhammad At Medina.* London, 1956.

Watt, W. Montgomery. *Islamic Political Thought.* Edinburgh, 1968.

Yafi'i, Abu Muhammad Abd Allah. *Mirat al-Jinan wa Ibrat al-Yaqzan.* Hyderabad 1337 AH.

Ya'qubi, Ahmad b. Ali Yaqub al-Wadih. *Al-Tarikh.* Beirut, 1960.

Yaqut, Shihab al-Din. *Mu'jam al-Buldan.* ed. Wutenfeld. Leipzig, 1868.

INDEX